The Case for Banning Pit-Bull Dogs: A Comprehensive Analysis for Politicians

Copyright Page

TITLE: The Case for Banning Pit-Bull Dogs: A Comprehensive Analysis for Politicians

1ST Edition

Copyright @ 2023

ISBN: 9798223750697

Table of Contents

The Case for Banning Pit-Bull Dogs: A Comprehensive Analysis for Politicians

By Roberto Miguel Rodriguez

Chapter 1: The reasons why pit-bull dogs should be BANNED!

The history and origins of pit-bull dogs

Subchapter: The History and Origins of Pit-Bull Dogs

Introduction:

Understanding the history and origins of pit-bull dogs is crucial in order to make informed decisions regarding their place in society. This subchapter aims to provide politicians with a comprehensive analysis of the breed's background, shedding light on their purpose and development over time.

Origins of the Breed:

Pit-bull dogs, a term encompassing several breeds such as the American Pit Bull Terrier, Staffordshire Bull Terrier, and American Staffordshire Terrier, trace their roots back to the early 19th century. Originally bred in England for bull-baiting and later for ratting, these dogs possessed strength, agility, and tenacity, characteristics essential for their intended purposes.

Evolution and Purpose:

As bull-baiting was eventually banned, pit-bull dogs found new roles in society. Immigrants brought them to America, where they were primarily used on farms to protect livestock and assist in hunting. Their loyalty, intelligence, and protective instincts made them ideal working dogs and beloved family companions.

Popularity and Controversy:

Over time, pit-bull dogs gained popularity due to their versatility and loving nature. However, their association with illegal dog fighting and irresponsible ownership has led to controversy and negative media portrayal. It is important to separate the actions of a few individuals from the breed as a whole and address the underlying issues.

Breed-Specific Legislation:

The implementation of breed-specific legislation (BSL) as a means to ban pit-bull dogs has been a topic of heated debate. Proponents argue that BSL is necessary to protect public safety, while opponents argue that it unfairly targets responsible owners and fails to address the root causes of dog aggression incidents.

Debunking Misconceptions:

It is essential to debunk myths and misconceptions surrounding pit-bull dogs. Scientific studies have consistently shown that breed alone is not a reliable predictor of aggression. Factors such as individual temperament, training, and socialization play a more significant role in a dog's behavior.

Ethical Concerns:

The ethical concerns surrounding pit-bull dog ownership revolve around responsible ownership and the prevention of dog aggression incidents. Advocating for responsible ownership, education, and training programs can address these concerns more effectively than a blanket breed ban.

Alternatives to Banning:

Instead of a complete ban, alternative solutions such as responsible ownership regulations, stricter penalties for irresponsible owners, and community-based initiatives can promote public safety while preserving the rights of responsible pit-bull dog owners.

Effectiveness of Breed-Specific Bans:

Examining the effectiveness of breed-specific bans in reducing dog bite incidents is crucial. Studies have shown that such bans often result in the displacement of the targeted breed, leading to the emergence of other potentially dangerous breeds. Comprehensive legislation focusing on responsible ownership and education has proven to be more effective in addressing dog aggression incidents.

Conclusion:

Understanding the history and origins of pit-bull dogs provides a foundation for informed decision-making regarding breed-specific legislation. By addressing the concerns surrounding pit-bull dogs, debunking myths, and exploring alternative solutions, politicians can make evidence-based decisions that prioritize public safety while preserving the rights of responsible pit-bull dog owners.

The physical characteristics and traits of pit-bull dogs

Understanding the physical characteristics and traits of pit-bull dogs is essential in comprehending the rationale behind the call for their ban. Pit-bull dogs, which include American Pit Bull Terriers, American Staffordshire Terriers, and Staffordshire Bull Terriers, possess distinct physical attributes and temperamental traits that set them apart from other dog breeds.

Physically, pit-bull dogs are medium-sized, muscular animals with powerful jaws and a sturdy build. They typically weigh between 30 to 80 pounds, with a height ranging from 17 to 21 inches at the shoulder. Their short, smooth coats come in various colors, adding to their visual appeal. These physical characteristics, combined with their high energy levels, make them formidable and potentially dangerous.

In terms of temperament, pit-bull dogs are often described as strong-willed, tenacious, and prone to dog aggression. While every dog is an individual and upbringing plays a significant role in behavior, pit-bull dogs have shown a propensity for displaying aggressive behavior towards other animals, particularly other dogs. This inherent trait, combined with their physical capabilities, underscores the potential danger they pose to public safety.

It is important to note that not all pit-bull dogs exhibit aggressive behavior. Responsible owners can train and socialize their dogs to be well-behaved members of society. However, the unpredictability of their nature, coupled with their physical prowess, makes it vital to consider the risks associated with these dogs when formulating policies related to public safety.

By understanding the physical characteristics and traits of pit-bull dogs, policymakers can make informed decisions regarding the ban on these breeds. It is crucial to prioritize public safety while also acknowledging the importance of responsible dog ownership. The aim should be to strike a balance that protects the community from potential harm without unfairly discriminating against responsible pit-bull dog owners.

In the following chapters, we will delve deeper into the impact of pit-bull dogs on public safety, explore the correlation between pit-bull dogs and dog aggression incidents, and discuss the effectiveness of breed-specific bans in reducing dog bite incidents. By examining these aspects, we can develop a comprehensive understanding of the need for and potential alternatives to banning pit-bull dogs.

The prevalence of pit-bull dog attacks and fatalities

The prevalence of pit-bull dog attacks and fatalities is a topic that cannot be ignored when discussing the need for a comprehensive analysis of pit-bull dog ownership and potential bans. As politicians, it is our responsibility to prioritize public safety and make informed decisions that protect our communities.

Statistics show that pit-bull dogs are responsible for a disproportionate number of attacks and fatalities compared to other dog breeds. According to the American Veterinary Medical Association, pit-bull type breeds account for a significant percentage of severe dog bite injuries and fatalities. These incidents often result in devastating consequences for victims, their families, and communities as a whole.

In recent years, the impact of pit-bull dog attacks on public safety has become increasingly evident. Numerous reports indicate that these attacks often involve more severe injuries and require extensive medical treatment. The emotional trauma experienced by victims can have long-lasting effects on their quality of life. It is our duty to protect our citizens from such harm and ensure their safety within their own neighborhoods.

Breed-specific legislation has been implemented in various jurisdictions as a means of addressing the issue. These laws target specific breeds, such as pit-bull dogs, in an effort to reduce the number of dog bite incidents. While controversial, breed-specific bans have shown some success in reducing the frequency of attacks in certain areas. However, the effectiveness of such legislation is still a subject of debate.

Debunking myths and misconceptions about pit-bull dogs is crucial in understanding the reasons behind their aggressive behavior. Contrary to popular belief, it is important to recognize that a dog's behavior is influenced by various factors, including training, socialization, and individual temperament. Blaming an entire breed for the actions of a few is both unfair and inaccurate.

The correlation between pit-bull dogs and dog aggression incidents cannot be ignored. While not all pit-bull dogs exhibit aggressive behavior, their genetic predisposition towards dog aggression is well-documented. This poses a risk not only to other dogs but also to their owners and the general public.

In addition to the emotional toll, pit-bull dog attacks also carry significant economic costs. Victims often require extensive medical treatment, which can result in substantial medical bills. Furthermore, legal battles and insurance claims can place a significant burden on both individuals and communities.

As politicians, we must explore potential alternatives to banning pit-bull dogs. This includes promoting responsible ownership, implementing stricter regulations, and increasing penalties for irresponsible owners. Education and awareness campaigns can also play a vital role in addressing the issue.

Lastly, it is essential to consider the impact of breed-specific bans on responsible pit-bull dog owners. While banning a breed may seem like a quick solution, it unfairly penalizes responsible owners who have taken the necessary steps to ensure their dogs are well-behaved members of society. Balancing the need for public safety with the rights of responsible owners is crucial in finding a comprehensive solution.

Media sensationalism plays a significant role in shaping public perception of pit-bull dogs. The biased portrayal of these dogs in the media often perpetuates stereotypes and fuels unnecessary fear. Encouraging accurate and balanced reporting can help dispel misconceptions surrounding pit-bull dogs.

In conclusion, exploring the effectiveness of breed-specific bans in reducing dog bite incidents is of utmost importance. The prevalence of pit-bull dog attacks and fatalities cannot be ignored, and as politicians, we must consider all aspects of this issue to make informed decisions that prioritize public safety and protect our communities.

The inherent breed-specific tendencies towards aggression

One of the primary arguments in favor of banning pit-bull dogs is their inherent breed-specific tendencies towards aggression. While it is important to acknowledge that not all pit-bull dogs exhibit aggressive behavior, statistics and studies consistently show that this particular breed has a higher propensity for aggression compared to other dog breeds.

Numerous studies have found that pit-bull dogs are responsible for a significant proportion of dog bite incidents, often resulting in severe injuries or even fatalities. Their strength, tenacity, and powerful jaw structure make them capable of inflicting devastating damage when they do attack. This breed-specific tendency towards aggression cannot be ignored, especially when it comes to public safety.

Breed-specific legislation (BSL) has been implemented in many jurisdictions as a means to address the issue of pit-bull dog aggression. By targeting specific breeds, such legislation aims to protect the public from potential harm. BSL typically includes measures such as mandatory spaying/neutering, strict containment requirements, and liability insurance for pit-bull dog owners.

Critics argue that BSL is ineffective and unfair, as it penalizes responsible pit-bull dog owners who have well-behaved pets. However, it is crucial to recognize that BSL is not a blanket solution but a response to a breed-specific problem. By focusing on pit-bull dogs, which have a higher likelihood of aggression, BSL can significantly reduce the incidence of dog bites and protect public safety.

It is important to debunk the myths and misconceptions surrounding pit-bull dogs to fully understand the breed-specific tendencies towards aggression. While some may argue that aggression is a result of poor training or mistreatment, studies consistently show that genetics play a significant role. The breed's history of being bred for dog fighting and its physical attributes contribute to its aggressive tendencies.

The ethical concerns surrounding pit-bull dog ownership are also important to consider. Owning a dog breed with a higher likelihood of aggression requires responsible ownership, including proper training, socialization, and secure containment. However, not all owners are capable or willing to meet these requirements, posing a risk to the community.

In conclusion, the inherent breed-specific tendencies towards aggression in pit-bull dogs cannot be ignored when addressing the issue of public safety. While not all pit-bull dogs exhibit aggressive behavior, the statistics and studies clearly indicate a higher propensity for aggression within this breed. Implementing breed-specific legislation targeted at pit-bull dogs is a reasonable and effective means to reduce dog bite incidents and protect the welfare of the community. Responsible pit-bull dog ownership should be encouraged, but public safety must remain the top priority.

The potential risks posed by pit-bull dogs to vulnerable populations

Title: The Potential Risks Posed by Pit-Bull Dogs to Vulnerable Populations

Introduction:

In this subchapter, we will delve into the potential risks that pit-bull dogs pose to vulnerable populations. As politicians, it is crucial to understand the implications of allowing these dogs within our communities. This section aims to provide a comprehensive analysis of the issues at hand, shedding light on the importance of considering a ban on pit-bull dogs.

1. Increased Threat to Public Safety:

Pit-bull dogs, with their powerful jaws and muscular build, have been associated with a higher risk of aggression towards humans. Studies have shown that their attacks are more severe and result in a higher number of fatalities and serious injuries. By banning pit-bull dogs, we can significantly reduce the threat they pose to our communities.

2. Breed-Specific Legislation and its Role:

Breed-specific legislation has proven effective in curbing dog-related incidents. By implementing targeted regulations, such as breed-specific bans, we can specifically address the risks posed by pit-bull dogs. These laws help protect vulnerable populations, ensuring public safety remains a priority.

3. Debunking Myths and Misconceptions:

It is important to separate fact from fiction when discussing pit-bull dogs. While some argue that responsible ownership can mitigate risks, research suggests that the breed's genetic predisposition to aggression cannot be easily eliminated. By addressing myths and misconceptions, we can make informed decisions based on evidence rather than emotions.

4. Ethical Concerns Surrounding Pit-Bull Dog Ownership:

The ethical considerations of owning pit-bull dogs must be evaluated. These dogs require experienced handlers and specific living conditions due to their inherent nature. By banning pit-bull dogs, we can prevent the unethical treatment of these animals and protect them from potential harm.

5. Economic Costs Associated with Pit-Bull Dog Attacks:

Dog attacks, particularly by pit-bull dogs, place a significant financial burden on communities. Costs include medical expenses, legal fees, and compensation for victims. By banning pit-bull dogs, we can alleviate this financial strain and redirect resources towards education and prevention programs.

Conclusion:

The potential risks posed by pit-bull dogs to vulnerable populations cannot be ignored. As politicians, it is our responsibility to prioritize public safety and make evidence-based decisions. By considering a ban on pit-bull dogs, we can protect our communities, address ethical concerns, and reduce the economic costs associated with dog attacks.

The limitations of training and socialization in mitigating aggression

When discussing the issue of pit-bull dogs and their potential danger to public safety, it is crucial to consider the limitations of training and socialization in mitigating aggression. While training and socialization play a vital role in shaping a dog's behavior, they are not foolproof methods for eliminating aggression, especially in certain breeds like pit-bulls.

Training and socialization are essential tools in teaching dogs how to behave appropriately in various situations. They help dogs learn basic obedience commands, develop good manners, and become well-adjusted members of society. However, it is important to acknowledge that these techniques have their limitations, particularly when dealing with breeds that have inherent aggressive tendencies.

Pit-bull dogs, often bred for their strength and tenacity, have a genetic predisposition towards aggression. Despite efforts to train and socialize them, their innate traits can still manifest in aggressive behavior. This is not to say that all pit-bull dogs are inherently aggressive, but rather that their potential for aggression is higher compared to many other breeds.

Furthermore, it is important to recognize that aggression in dogs can be influenced by various factors, including genetics, environment, and individual experiences. Training and socialization can only go so far in mitigating aggression when these underlying factors are present.

While responsible ownership and proper training can help mitigate aggression to some extent, it is unrealistic to rely solely on these methods for public safety. Breed-specific legislation, such as banning pit-bull dogs, can provide an additional layer of protection for communities. By implementing breed-specific bans, policymakers can prioritize public safety by reducing the risk of dog aggression incidents involving pit-bulls.

It is imperative for politicians to understand that training and socialization are not foolproof solutions for addressing aggression, particularly in breeds with genetic predispositions towards aggression like pit-bulls. By acknowledging these limitations, policymakers can make informed decisions regarding breed-specific legislation and prioritize public safety over potential risks associated with certain dog breeds.

The responsibility of society to prioritize public safety over individual preferences

In today's society, the safety and well-being of the public should always take precedence over individual preferences. This is especially true when it comes to the controversial issue of pit-bull dogs and their impact on public safety. While pit-bull dogs have their loyal supporters who argue against their banning, the evidence and data overwhelmingly support the need for prioritizing public safety.

The impact of pit-bull dogs on public safety cannot be ignored. Numerous studies have shown that pit-bull dogs are responsible for a significant number of dog attacks and fatalities. Their inherent strength and tenacity make them more prone to causing severe injuries, particularly when compared to other dog breeds. The statistics speak for themselves, and it is essential for society to acknowledge and address this issue.

Breed-specific legislation plays a vital role in pit-bull dog bans. By implementing laws that specifically target pit-bull dogs, policymakers can effectively reduce the number of dog bite incidents. These laws ensure that potential dangers are identified and controlled, preventing future tragedies from occurring. While some argue against breed-specific legislation, it is important to recognize that these laws are not targeting responsible dog owners but rather focusing on the breed's potential risks.

Debunking myths and misconceptions about pit-bull dogs is crucial in shaping public perception. Many people believe that pit-bull dogs are inherently aggressive and dangerous. However, research has shown that a dog's behavior is primarily influenced by its upbringing and environment. By challenging these misconceptions, society can move towards a more informed and rational understanding of pit-bull dogs.

The economic costs associated with pit-bull dog attacks cannot be overlooked. These attacks often result in expensive medical bills, legal fees, and compensation claims. By prioritizing public safety and banning pit-bull dogs, society can significantly reduce these financial burdens on individuals and the healthcare system.

While banning pit-bull dogs may seem extreme to some, there are potential alternatives to consider. These alternatives include stricter regulations and licensing requirements for pit-bull dog ownership, mandatory training and socialization programs, and increased enforcement of existing dog control laws. By implementing these measures, society can strike a balance between individual preferences and public safety.

In conclusion, the responsibility of society to prioritize public safety over individual preferences is paramount when it comes to the issue of pit-bull dogs. The evidence overwhelmingly supports the need for banning pit-bull dogs to reduce dog bite incidents and protect the well-being of the public. By implementing breed-specific legislation and challenging misconceptions, society can work towards a safer and more informed approach to pit-bull dog ownership. It is crucial for policymakers to consider the impact of breed-specific bans on responsible dog owners and explore alternative measures to ensure public safety. Ultimately, the goal should be to strike a balance between individual preferences and the greater good of society.

Chapter 2: The impact of pit-bull dogs on public safety

The frequency and severity of pit-bull dog attacks

In recent years, there has been a growing concern regarding the frequency and severity of pit-bull dog attacks. These incidents have resulted in numerous injuries and, in some cases, even fatalities. This subchapter aims to shed light on the alarming statistics surrounding pit-bull dog attacks and highlight the need for immediate action in the form of a ban on these dangerous animals.

Statistics from reputable sources such as the Centers for Disease Control and Prevention (CDC) and the American Veterinary Medical Association (AVMA) reveal a troubling trend. Pit-bull dogs consistently rank at the top of the list when it comes to dog attacks, accounting for a significant percentage of reported incidents. These attacks are often characterized by their severity, involving multiple bites and causing extensive damage to victims, both physically and psychologically.

Furthermore, studies have shown that pit-bull dogs are responsible for a disproportionate number of fatal attacks on humans compared to other dog breeds. This raises serious concerns about public safety and the potential risk these dogs pose to communities. It is crucial for politicians to acknowledge these statistics and take decisive action to protect their constituents.

Critics argue that breed-specific legislation unfairly targets pit-bull dogs and their owners. However, it is important to recognize that breed-specific bans have been proven effective in reducing dog bite incidents in various jurisdictions. These laws aim to prevent future attacks by targeting the source of the problem rather than penalizing all dog owners. By implementing breed-specific legislation, politicians can strike a balance between public safety and individual rights.

Debunking myths and misconceptions surrounding pit-bull dogs is essential in this discussion. Contrary to popular belief, these attacks are not solely the result of irresponsible ownership or mistreatment. Pit-bull dogs have a genetic predisposition towards aggression, making them more prone to attack than other breeds. This is not a reflection of individual dogs' personalities but rather an inherent characteristic of the breed.

The frequency and severity of pit-bull dog attacks not only pose a threat to public safety but also result in significant economic costs. Medical expenses, legal fees, and compensation for victims can quickly escalate, burdening communities and taxpayers. By implementing a ban on pit-bull dogs, politicians can alleviate these financial burdens and redirect resources towards more pressing issues.

In conclusion, the frequency and severity of pit-bull dog attacks demand immediate attention from politicians. The statistics speak for themselves, highlighting the need for a ban on these dangerous animals. By taking decisive action, politicians can ensure public safety, protect communities, and reduce the economic costs associated with these attacks. The time for action is now, and a comprehensive analysis of the impact of pit-bull dogs on public safety supports the case for their banning.

The psychological and physical trauma experienced by victims

The psychological and physical trauma experienced by victims is a critical aspect that cannot be overlooked when discussing the need for banning pit-bull dogs. This subchapter aims to shed light on the devastating impact that these dogs can have on individuals and communities.

Victims of pit-bull dog attacks often endure severe physical injuries that can be life-altering. The powerful jaws and muscular build of these dogs can cause deep tissue damage, extensive lacerations, and even limb amputations. The physical recovery from such injuries can be arduous and may require multiple surgeries and long-term rehabilitation. In some cases, victims are left with permanent disfigurement, chronic pain, and mobility issues.

Beyond the physical injuries, the psychological trauma experienced by victims is equally distressing. Survivors of pit-bull attacks often suffer from post-traumatic stress disorder (PTSD), anxiety disorders, and depression. The viciousness of these attacks can leave victims with a heightened sense of fear and vulnerability, making it difficult for them to resume normal activities or interact with dogs in the future. The emotional scars can last a lifetime and have a profound impact on their overall well-being.

Not only do victims suffer individually, but the trauma also extends to their families and communities. Witnessing a loved one being viciously attacked by a pit-bull dog can lead to a sense of helplessness and guilt among family members. Communities may also experience a decline in public safety perception, as residents fear similar attacks and the potential for more victims.

Addressing the psychological and physical trauma experienced by victims is crucial in advocating for a ban on pit-bull dogs. By taking decisive action to prohibit the ownership of these breeds, politicians can ensure the safety and well-being of their constituents. Banning pit-bull dogs can prevent future incidents, protect innocent individuals from harm, and alleviate the burden on healthcare systems and support services.

In conclusion, the psychological and physical trauma experienced by victims of pit-bull dog attacks is a significant concern that demands immediate attention. By recognizing the devastating impact on individuals, families, and communities, politicians can make informed decisions to protect public safety and prevent future tragedies. Banning pit-bull dogs is a necessary step towards mitigating the psychological and physical trauma inflicted upon victims and ensuring a safer environment for all.

The strain on emergency medical services and hospitals

The strain on emergency medical services and hospitals is a significant concern when it comes to pit-bull dog attacks. These attacks often result in severe injuries that require immediate medical attention, putting a strain on emergency rooms and hospitals.

Pit-bull dogs are known for their strong jaws and tenacious nature, which can lead to more severe injuries compared to other dog breeds. Their bites often result in deep puncture wounds, torn flesh, and broken bones. These injuries require extensive medical treatment, including surgeries, wound care, and rehabilitation.

Emergency medical services are often the first responders to pit-bull dog attacks. These professionals are faced with the challenging task of stabilizing victims and transporting them to hospitals for further treatment. The increasing frequency of pit-bull dog attacks puts a burden on these services, stretching their resources and limiting their ability to respond to other emergencies in a timely manner.

Hospitals also face challenges in dealing with the aftermath of pit-bull dog attacks. These attacks often result in extended hospital stays and the need for specialized medical interventions. The cost of treating these injuries can be substantial, placing an additional burden on healthcare systems.

Furthermore, the strain on emergency medical services and hospitals extends beyond the immediate aftermath of an attack. Victims of pit-bull dog attacks may require ongoing medical care, including reconstructive surgeries and psychological counseling to cope with the trauma. This long-term care can further strain healthcare resources and impact the overall quality of care provided to other patients.

Addressing the strain on emergency medical services and hospitals requires a comprehensive approach. Implementing breed-specific legislation can help reduce the number of pit-bull dog attacks and alleviate the burden on healthcare systems. By banning pit-bull dogs, policymakers can protect public safety and ensure that emergency medical services and hospitals can effectively respond to emergencies without being overwhelmed.

In conclusion, the strain on emergency medical services and hospitals caused by pit-bull dog attacks is a pressing issue that demands attention. Banning pit-bull dogs can help alleviate this strain and ensure that healthcare resources are available to all members of the community.

The emotional toll on communities affected by pit-bull dog attacks

Introduction:

Pit-bull dog attacks have long been a cause for concern, and the emotional toll they take on communities cannot be overlooked. This subchapter aims to shed light on the deep-rooted emotional impact that pit-bull dog attacks have on affected communities. By understanding this aspect, politicians can make informed decisions about the need to implement breed-specific legislation and ultimately ban pit-bull dogs.

Emotional Trauma:

The aftermath of a pit-bull dog attack leaves victims and their communities grappling with profound emotional trauma. The physical injuries sustained during these attacks are often severe, resulting in long-lasting scars, both physically and emotionally. Victims may suffer from post-traumatic stress disorder, anxiety, and depression. Witnessing such attacks can also traumatize bystanders, exacerbating the emotional toll on the community.

Fear and Distrust:

Pit-bull dog attacks create an atmosphere of fear and distrust within communities. Parents become reluctant to let their children play outside, and individuals are hesitant to walk their dogs in fear of encountering an aggressive pit-bull. This fear and distrust can lead to a breakdown in community cohesion and a diminished sense of safety, affecting the quality of life for residents.

Grief and Loss:

Communities affected by pit-bull dog attacks also experience grief and loss. The loss of a loved one or a cherished pet in a pit-bull attack is devastating. The emotional pain and grief experienced by families and friends cannot be quantified. These tragic incidents leave a lasting impact on the community, with painful reminders of the lives lost.

Support and Rehabilitation:

It is essential to recognize the emotional toll and provide support for affected communities. This support can come in the form of counseling services, support groups, and resources to help victims cope with the trauma. Additionally, rehabilitation programs for aggressive dogs can play a pivotal role in preventing future attacks and helping communities heal.

Conclusion:

The emotional toll on communities affected by pit-bull dog attacks is significant and cannot be underestimated. The fear, distrust, grief, and loss experienced by victims and their communities have a profound impact on their well-being and quality of life. Politicians must consider the emotional aspect when evaluating the need for breed-specific legislation and the ultimate ban on pit-bull dogs. By prioritizing public safety and the emotional well-being of their constituents, politicians can make informed decisions that protect communities from the devastating consequences of pit-bull dog attacks.

The fear and anxiety created by the presence of pit-bull dogs in neighborhoods

The fear and anxiety created by the presence of pit-bull dogs in neighborhoods is a topic that has sparked heated debates and divided communities. This subchapter aims to shed light on the reasons why pit-bull dogs should be banned, particularly from the perspective of politicians who play a crucial role in shaping public policy.

Firstly, it is essential to recognize the impact of pit-bull dogs on public safety. Numerous studies have shown that pit-bull dogs are responsible for a disproportionate number of severe and fatal dog attacks. This breed is known for its powerful jaws and tenacious nature, making them more prone to inflicting serious injuries. By banning pit-bull dogs, neighborhoods can significantly reduce the risk of such attacks and ensure the safety of their residents.

Breed-specific legislation (BSL) is one approach that has been implemented by many jurisdictions to regulate or ban specific dog breeds. This subchapter will explore the role of BSL in pit-bull dog bans and its effectiveness in reducing dog bite incidents. While critics argue that BSL unfairly targets certain breeds, proponents argue that it is a necessary measure to protect public safety.

Debunking myths and misconceptions about pit-bull dogs is another crucial aspect to consider. Many people believe that pit-bull dogs are inherently aggressive and dangerous, but research has shown that breed alone is not a reliable predictor of aggression. By providing accurate and evidence-based information, politicians can help dispel these misconceptions and promote a more informed debate on pit-bull dog bans.

Ethical concerns surrounding pit-bull dog ownership must also be addressed. Some argue that banning a specific breed infringes on individuals' rights to choose the type of dog they want to own. However, the potential harm that pit-bull dogs can cause to humans and other animals must be weighed against these concerns, ultimately prioritizing public safety.

Furthermore, exploring the economic costs associated with pit-bull dog attacks can provide politicians with additional motivation for implementing breed-specific bans. Medical expenses, legal battles, and the impact on insurance rates are just a few aspects to consider.

Lastly, this subchapter will touch upon the potential alternatives to banning pit-bull dogs, such as stricter regulations, mandatory training, and responsible ownership programs. By considering these alternatives, politicians can strike a balance between public safety and individual rights.

In conclusion, the fear and anxiety created by the presence of pit-bull dogs in neighborhoods demand serious attention from politicians. By thoroughly analyzing the impact of pit-bull dogs on public safety, debunking myths, and addressing ethical concerns, politicians can make informed decisions regarding breed-specific bans. The ultimate goal is to ensure the well-being and safety of communities while also considering alternative solutions that balance individual rights.

The negative impact on tourism and local economies

In addition to the concerns surrounding public safety and the ethical concerns surrounding pit-bull dog ownership, there is also a significant negative impact on tourism and local economies caused by these dogs. This subchapter aims to shed light on this aspect of the pit-bull dog issue, providing politicians with a comprehensive understanding of the economic implications associated with these breeds.

One of the key concerns is the effect that pit-bull dogs have on tourism. Many potential visitors, especially families with children, are hesitant to travel to destinations where these dogs are prevalent due to the perceived danger they pose. This fear can lead to a decline in tourism, resulting in significant financial losses for local economies heavily reliant on tourism revenue.

Moreover, the presence of pit-bull dogs in a community can also deter potential investors and businesses. Entrepreneurs and investors may be reluctant to establish businesses or invest in areas where there is a perceived risk associated with these breeds. This reluctance can stifle economic growth and development, leading to missed opportunities for job creation and economic prosperity.

Furthermore, the economic costs associated with pit-bull dog attacks are substantial. These attacks can result in significant medical expenses for victims, including emergency room visits, surgeries, and ongoing rehabilitation. These costs often fall on the public healthcare system, putting a strain on limited resources and diverting funds that could be allocated to other pressing healthcare needs.

Additionally, these attacks can lead to legal battles, further burdening the already overwhelmed judicial system. Lawsuits stemming from pit-bull dog attacks can result in significant financial settlements and legal fees, putting a strain on local governments and taxpayers.

By addressing the negative impact on tourism and local economies, politicians can better understand the broader implications of the pit-bull dog issue. This understanding can inform their decision-making processes and enable them to develop comprehensive policies that not only prioritize public safety and ethical concerns but also consider the economic wellbeing of their constituents. It is crucial for politicians to acknowledge the economic consequences and seek viable solutions that strike a balance between the interests of responsible pit-bull dog owners and the overall welfare of their communities.

Chapter 3: The role of breed-specific legislation in pit-bull dog bans

The definition and purpose of breed-specific legislation (BSL)

In recent years, the issue of pit-bull dogs and their impact on public safety has become a topic of great concern. As politicians, it is our duty to address this issue and take appropriate action to protect our communities. One potential solution that has gained attention is breed-specific legislation (BSL). This subchapter aims to provide a comprehensive understanding of BSL, its purpose, and its potential implications.

BSL can be defined as a set of laws or regulations that target specific dog breeds, often including pit-bull dogs, with the aim of reducing dog bite incidents and enhancing public safety. These laws often involve restrictions on ownership, mandatory spaying/neutering, liability insurance, and even outright bans on certain breeds.

The primary purpose of BSL is to address the perceived inherent dangers associated with certain dog breeds, particularly pit-bull dogs. Advocates argue that these breeds have a higher propensity for aggression, which poses a significant risk to public safety. By implementing breed-specific bans or regulations, policymakers aim to mitigate these risks and protect their constituents.

However, it is essential to critically evaluate the effectiveness and ethical implications of BSL. Critics argue that singling out specific breeds is an unfair and ineffective approach to dog bite prevention. They contend that focusing on individual dog behavior and responsible ownership practices would yield better results. Furthermore, opponents of BSL argue that it unfairly stigmatizes responsible pit-bull dog owners who have well-behaved and loving pets.

This subchapter will delve into the various arguments surrounding BSL, addressing both the perspectives of those advocating for pit-bull dog bans and those opposing them. It will examine the correlation between pit-bull dogs and dog aggression incidents, exploring whether breed-specific bans effectively reduce such incidents. Additionally, it will shed light on the economic costs associated with pit-bull dog attacks and discuss potential alternatives to outright bans, such as education, stricter penalties for irresponsible owners, and breed-neutral legislation.

By understanding the definition and purpose of BSL, we can better evaluate its effectiveness, ethical implications, and potential alternatives. As policymakers, it is crucial to make informed decisions that balance public safety concerns with the rights of responsible pet owners. Through a comprehensive analysis of BSL, we can work towards creating policies that protect our communities while respecting the rights of all dog owners.

The effectiveness of BSL in reducing pit-bull dog attacks

Breed-specific legislation (BSL) has been a contentious topic in the realm of dog ownership and public safety. Many argue that BSL unfairly targets certain breeds, such as pit-bull dogs, while others contend that it is a necessary measure to protect communities from dog attacks. In this subchapter, we will delve into the effectiveness of BSL specifically in reducing pit-bull dog attacks, providing a comprehensive analysis for politicians.

Evidence suggests that BSL can indeed be effective in reducing pit-bull dog attacks. Numerous studies have shown a correlation between breed-specific bans and a decrease in dog bite incidents involving pit-bull dogs. For example, a study conducted in Denver, Colorado, found that after implementing a ban on pit-bull dogs in 1989, the number of pit-bull dog attacks decreased significantly. Similar results have been observed in other jurisdictions that have implemented BSL targeting pit-bull dogs.

BSL can be effective because it addresses the inherent characteristics and traits that make certain breeds more prone to aggression. Pit-bull dogs, in particular, have a strong prey drive and a powerful bite force, which can make them more dangerous in certain situations. By implementing BSL, lawmakers can regulate and control the ownership and breeding of pit-bull dogs, thereby reducing the likelihood of attacks.

Critics of BSL argue that it unfairly stigmatizes certain breeds and punishes responsible dog owners. However, it is important to note that BSL does not necessarily equate to a total ban on pit-bull dogs. Many jurisdictions have adopted a tiered approach, where pit-bull owners are required to adhere to specific regulations and requirements, such as mandatory spaying/neutering, liability insurance, and secure containment.

Furthermore, BSL should not be viewed as a standalone solution to the issue of dog attacks. It should be complemented with comprehensive education and responsible ownership programs. By promoting responsible pet ownership and educating the public about the potential risks associated with certain breeds, communities can further mitigate the occurrence of dog attacks.

In conclusion, breed-specific legislation can be an effective tool in reducing pit-bull dog attacks. While it may be a controversial measure, evidence suggests that it has yielded positive results in jurisdictions where it has been implemented. However, it is crucial for lawmakers to strike a balance between public safety and responsible dog ownership, ensuring that BSL is implemented in a fair and targeted manner. By doing so, communities can create a safer environment for their residents while still respecting the rights of responsible pit-bull dog owners.

The legal and constitutional considerations surrounding BSL

The legal and constitutional considerations surrounding Breed-Specific Legislation (BSL) are crucial in understanding the broader implications of pit-bull dog bans. As politicians, it is essential to be well-informed about the legal framework and constitutional rights that come into play when discussing BSL. This subchapter aims to provide a comprehensive analysis of these considerations, shedding light on the complexities and potential pitfalls associated with enacting breed-specific bans.

First and foremost, it is important to recognize that BSL raises significant legal and constitutional concerns. Critics argue that breed-specific bans may infringe upon the rights of responsible pit-bull dog owners, as well as violate principles of equal protection under the law. Implementing a ban based solely on breed can be seen as discriminatory and arbitrary, as it targets a specific type of dog without considering the individual temperament or behavior of each animal.

Furthermore, the constitutionality of BSL has been a subject of debate in many jurisdictions. Courts have often questioned the rational basis for singling out pit-bull dogs, emphasizing the lack of scientific evidence linking breed to aggression. In some cases, breed-specific bans have been challenged and overturned on constitutional grounds, highlighting the need for careful consideration when crafting legislation.

Additionally, legal challenges can arise from the enforcement of BSL. Determining the breed of a dog can be subjective and prone to error, leading to potential legal disputes. It is essential to establish clear guidelines and definitions to avoid confusion and ensure fair treatment for all dog owners.

Moreover, the potential impact on responsible pit-bull dog owners cannot be overlooked. Many individuals have formed strong emotional bonds with their pets and consider them a part of their families. BSL can lead to the forced separation or euthanization of beloved pets, causing immense distress and hardship for responsible owners who have not caused harm.

In conclusion, the legal and constitutional considerations surrounding BSL are multifaceted and demand careful examination. While public safety is undoubtedly a priority, it is crucial to balance this with the protection of individual rights and the avoidance of discriminatory practices. As politicians, it is essential to approach the issue of pit-bull dog bans with a deep understanding of the legal complexities, ensuring that any legislation is fair, effective, and in line with constitutional principles.

The experiences of cities and countries that have implemented BSL

The experiences of cities and countries that have implemented Breed-Specific Legislation (BSL) provide valuable insights into the effectiveness and impact of such measures. By examining the outcomes of BSL implementation, policymakers can make informed decisions about whether to ban pit-bull dogs in their jurisdiction.

One of the most notable cities to implement BSL is Denver, Colorado. In 1989, the city passed a ban on pit-bull dogs, making it illegal to own or keep them within city limits. Over the years, Denver has reported a significant decrease in dog bite incidents involving pit-bull dogs. This suggests that BSL can effectively reduce the number of dog attacks and enhance public safety.

Similarly, the province of Ontario, Canada, enacted BSL in 2005, which included a ban on pit-bull dogs. Since then, Ontario has observed a decline in the number of pit-bull-related incidents, reinforcing the notion that BSL can have a positive impact on public safety.

Contrary to popular misconceptions, the experiences of cities and countries with BSL demonstrate that these measures do not lead to the mass euthanization of pit-bull dogs. Many jurisdictions that have implemented BSL have included provisions for responsible pit-bull dog owners to keep their pets under certain conditions. This approach allows for the protection of public safety while still showing sensitivity towards responsible dog ownership.

Additionally, the economic costs associated with pit-bull dog attacks can be significant. By implementing BSL, cities and countries can potentially reduce the financial burden on their healthcare systems and animal control services. The resources saved can then be diverted to other important areas, such as education, infrastructure, or healthcare.

Overall, the experiences of cities and countries that have implemented BSL provide compelling evidence in support of banning pit-bull dogs. These measures have been shown to effectively reduce dog bite incidents and enhance public safety without leading to the mass euthanization of these animals. By learning from these experiences, policymakers can make informed decisions that prioritize the well-being and safety of their constituents.

The potential alternatives to BSL in addressing pit-bull dog issues

While many argue for the implementation of Breed-Specific Legislation (BSL) as a means to address pit-bull dog issues, it is important to consider alternative approaches that may be more effective and fair to responsible dog owners. BSL, while targeting specific breeds, fails to address the root causes of dog aggression incidents and can unfairly stigmatize pit-bull dogs and their owners. In this subchapter, we will explore some potential alternatives to BSL that can effectively address the concerns surrounding pit-bull dogs.

1. Education and Responsible Ownership Programs: Instead of targeting specific breeds, efforts should be invested in educating dog owners about responsible ownership practices. This can include mandatory training

and behavior classes, licensing and registration requirements, and promoting responsible breeding practices. By focusing on responsible ownership, we can ensure that all dog owners, regardless of breed, are equipped with the knowledge and skills to prevent dog aggression incidents.

2. Enhanced Animal Control Measures: Implementing and enforcing stricter animal control measures can help address dog aggression issues more effectively. This can include increased penalties for owners whose dogs are involved in aggressive incidents, mandatory reporting of such incidents, and improved enforcement of existing leash laws and public safety regulations. By holding owners accountable for their dogs' behavior, we can target the problem at its source instead of unfairly targeting specific breeds.

3. Community Outreach and Support: Establishing community programs that promote responsible pet ownership and provide resources and support to dog owners can also be an effective alternative to BSL. These programs can include low-cost spay/neuter clinics, free or discounted training classes, and outreach efforts to underserved communities. By providing accessible resources and support, we can help prevent dog aggression incidents and promote a safer community for all.

4. Data-Driven Policies: Instead of relying on breed stereotypes, policymakers should consider evidence-based approaches that focus on individual dog behavior and owner responsibility. By analyzing comprehensive data on dog attacks, we can identify the factors that contribute to aggressive behavior and implement targeted interventions that address those factors.

In conclusion, there are alternative approaches to BSL that can effectively address pit-bull dog issues without unfairly targeting specific breeds. By focusing on education, responsible ownership programs, enhanced animal control measures, community outreach, and data-driven policies, we can promote a safer and more inclusive approach to dog-related issues. It is crucial for policymakers to consider these alternatives and work towards policies that prioritize public safety while respecting the rights of responsible pit-bull dog owners.

The importance of comprehensive and well-enforced legislation

The importance of comprehensive and well-enforced legislation cannot be overstated when it comes to addressing the issue of pit-bull dogs. In order to effectively protect public safety and mitigate the risks associated with this breed, it is crucial for politicians to enact laws that specifically target pit-bull dogs. This subchapter will delve into the reasons why comprehensive and well-enforced legislation is essential in addressing this issue.

Firstly, comprehensive legislation allows for a clear definition of what constitutes a pit-bull dog, ensuring that there is no ambiguity or confusion surrounding the breed. This is crucial because it enables law enforcement agencies and animal control officers to easily identify pit-bull dogs and enforce the regulations in place. Without such legislation, it becomes difficult to implement any meaningful regulations or restrictions on this breed.

Furthermore, well-enforced legislation acts as a deterrent for potential pit-bull dog owners who may not be responsible or capable of properly handling these dogs. By imposing strict regulations and penalties, politicians can discourage individuals from owning pit-bull dogs unless they are well-prepared to meet the responsibilities that come with it. This helps to prevent cases of negligence or improper care, thereby reducing the risks associated with owning this breed.

Comprehensive and well-enforced legislation also plays a crucial role in protecting public safety. By implementing breed-specific regulations, politicians can ensure that pit-bull dogs are properly controlled and managed. This can include requirements such as mandatory spaying/neutering, leash and muzzle laws, and strict licensing and registration processes. Such regulations are aimed at reducing the chances of aggressive behavior and preventing potential incidents involving pit-bull dogs.

In addition, comprehensive legislation can address the concerns surrounding the ethical implications of owning pit-bull dogs. By imposing restrictions and regulations, politicians can ensure that potential owners are thoroughly educated on the breed's specific needs, characteristics, and potential risks. This helps to promote responsible ownership and prevent cases of mistreatment or neglect.

Overall, comprehensive and well-enforced legislation is of utmost importance in addressing the issues associated with pit-bull dogs. By enacting laws that specifically target this breed, politicians can protect public safety, mitigate risks, and promote responsible ownership. It is essential for politicians to recognize the significance of such legislation and take decisive action to address this pressing issue.

Chapter 4: Debunking myths and misconceptions about pit-bull dogs

The impact of media portrayal on public perception

In the age of information overload, the media plays a crucial role in shaping public perception on various issues, including the controversial topic of pit-bull dogs. The way pit-bull dogs are portrayed in the media has a significant impact on how the general public perceives these animals and influences the ongoing debate on their banning. It is imperative for politicians to understand this influence and critically analyze the media's role in shaping public opinion.

The media's portrayal of pit-bull dogs often focuses on sensationalized stories of attacks and aggression, creating a skewed perception that these dogs are inherently dangerous and unpredictable. This portrayal perpetuates the misconception that all pit-bull dogs are vicious, leading to widespread fear and calls for banning them. However, it is essential to recognize that sensationalism and selective reporting contribute to this biased perception.

By focusing solely on negative incidents involving pit-bull dogs, the media fails to provide a comprehensive understanding of the breed. Numerous studies have shown that a dog's behavior is primarily influenced by its upbringing, training, and environment, rather than its breed. However, the media's portrayal tends to overlook these factors, leading to an inaccurate representation of pit-bull dogs and reinforcing existing prejudices.

Politicians must be aware that media sensationalism can have severe consequences, not only for pit-bull dogs but also for responsible owners and communities as a whole. Misleading media coverage can lead to breed-specific legislation, which unfairly targets responsible dog owners based on the breed they choose to own. This type of legislation fails to address the root causes of dog aggression and can result in the euthanization of perfectly well-behaved animals.

To combat the negative impact of media portrayal, politicians should advocate for responsible reporting and balanced representation of pit-bull dogs. It is crucial to educate the public about the complexities of dog behavior and emphasize responsible ownership practices. By promoting accurate information and dispelling myths surrounding pit-bull dogs, politicians can help shape a more informed and rational public perception.

In conclusion, the media's portrayal of pit-bull dogs has a profound impact on public perception and influences the ongoing debate on their banning. Politicians must recognize this influence and work towards promoting responsible reporting and accurate information. By doing so, they can foster a more balanced and informed discussion on pit-bull dogs, ultimately leading to more effective policies that prioritize public safety while respecting the rights of responsible dog owners.

Separating fact from fiction: dispelling common misconceptions

Subchapter: Separating Fact from Fiction: Dispelling Common Misconceptions

Introduction:

In the contentious debate surrounding the banning of pit-bull dogs, it is crucial for politicians to base their decisions on accurate information rather than perpetuating myths and misconceptions. This subchapter aims to debunk some of the most common misunderstandings about pit-bull dogs, providing a comprehensive analysis for politicians who seek a fair evaluation of this issue.

1. The Reasons Why Pit-Bull Dogs Should Be Banned!

Before exploring the misconceptions, it is important to understand the arguments put forth in favor of banning pit-bull dogs. This section provides a comprehensive overview of the concerns related to public safety, ethical concerns, economic costs, and the potential alternatives to banning.

2. The Impact of Pit-Bull Dogs on Public Safety

This section delves into the statistical data surrounding dog bite incidents, examining whether pit-bull dogs are indeed more dangerous than other breeds. It also evaluates the impact of responsible ownership and socialization on a dog's behavior.

3. The Role of Breed-Specific Legislation in Pit-Bull Dog Bans

Examining the effectiveness of breed-specific legislation (BSL) in reducing dog bite incidents, this section highlights the limitations and unintended consequences of targeting specific breeds. It presents alternative approaches that prioritize responsible pet ownership and education.

4. Debunking Myths and Misconceptions about Pit-Bull Dogs

Addressing common misconceptions surrounding pit-bull dogs, this section provides evidence-based facts to counter arguments such as their inherent aggression, locking jaws, and unpredictability. It emphasizes the importance of individual dog assessment rather than generalizing based on breed.

5. The Ethical Concerns Surrounding Pit-Bull Dog Ownership

Exploring the ethical implications of breed-specific bans, this section questions the fairness of punishing responsible owners and well-behaved dogs based solely on breed stereotypes. It highlights the need for ethical and compassionate legislation that focuses on individual behavior.

6. The Correlation between Pit-Bull Dogs and Dog Aggression Incidents

This section examines scientific studies to determine if there is a direct correlation between pit-bull dogs and higher rates of aggression. It also discusses the factors that contribute to dog aggression and challenges the assumption that breed alone is a reliable predictor.

7. The Economic Costs Associated with Pit-Bull Dog Attacks

Analyzing the financial impact of dog attacks, this section evaluates whether the economic burden justifies breed-specific bans. It also explores alternative solutions, such as stricter regulations for all dog breeds, that may be more cost-effective.

8. The Potential Alternatives to Banning Pit-Bull Dogs

Presenting alternatives to complete bans, this section explores comprehensive approaches such as responsible ownership education, mandatory training and socialization, and stricter regulations for all dog breeds. It emphasizes the need for evidence-based policies that prioritize public safety without unfairly targeting specific breeds.

9. The Impact of Breed-Specific Bans on Responsible Pit-Bull Dog Owners

Examining the unintended consequences of breed-specific bans on responsible owners, this section highlights how such legislation can lead to discrimination, forced rehoming, or euthanasia of well-behaved dogs. It emphasizes the importance of balanced regulations that protect responsible ownership rights.

10. The Role of Media Sensationalism in Shaping Public Perception of Pit-Bull Dogs

This section examines the influence of media sensationalism on public perception of pit-bull dogs, exploring how biased reporting can perpetuate stereotypes and misconceptions. It emphasizes the need for accurate and balanced media representation to inform public opinion and decision-making.

11. Exploring the Effectiveness of Breed-Specific Bans in Reducing Dog Bite Incidents

This section critically evaluates the effectiveness of breed-specific bans in reducing dog bite incidents, examining case studies and comparing them to alternative approaches. It highlights the importance of evidence-based policies that prioritize public safety without targeting specific breeds.

Conclusion:

Dispelling common misconceptions surrounding pit-bull dogs is crucial for politicians to make fair and informed decisions regarding breed-specific bans. By examining the facts, exploring alternative solutions, and considering the ethical implications, policymakers can move towards legislation that prioritizes public safety, responsible ownership, and evidence-based approaches.

Understanding the role of responsible ownership in dog behavior

Introduction:

In order to have a comprehensive analysis of the issue of banning pit-bull dogs, it is essential to understand the role of responsible ownership in dog behavior. Responsible ownership plays a crucial role in shaping a dog's behavior and preventing incidents of aggression. This subchapter aims to shed light on the importance of responsible ownership and its impact on dog behavior, specifically in the context of pit-bull dogs.

Responsible Ownership and Dog Behavior:

Responsible ownership encompasses factors such as proper training, socialization, and adherence to community regulations. When owners take the initiative to provide their dogs with appropriate training and socialization, they can significantly influence their behavior. Pit-bull dogs, like any other breed, can be well-behaved and friendly when raised in a responsible and caring environment.

The Role of Education and Training:

Education and training are key components of responsible ownership. By providing owners with the necessary knowledge and skills to understand and handle their dogs, we can prevent behavioral issues from arising. Educating owners about a dog's needs, temperament, and behavior can help them develop a strong bond with their pets and address any potential issues before they escalate.

Promoting Responsible Ownership:

As policymakers, it is essential to focus on promoting responsible ownership rather than imposing breed-specific bans. Encouraging owners to enroll their dogs in obedience classes, providing resources for training, and offering incentives for responsible ownership can have a positive impact on dog behavior and public safety.

Collaboration with Animal Welfare Organizations:

Working closely with animal welfare organizations can also contribute to responsible ownership. These organizations can provide support, resources, and guidance to dog owners, ensuring that they have the necessary tools to raise well-behaved and safe dogs. By fostering a collaborative approach, we can create a positive and supportive environment for responsible dog ownership.

Conclusion:

Understanding the role of responsible ownership in dog behavior is crucial when considering whether to ban specific breeds such as pit-bull dogs. Responsible ownership, through education, training, and collaboration, can significantly impact a dog's behavior and prevent incidents of aggression. Instead of focusing solely on breed-specific bans, policymakers should prioritize promoting responsible ownership as a more effective and ethical approach to ensuring public safety. By doing so, we can foster a society where all dogs, including pit-bull dogs, can coexist safely and harmoniously with humans.

The importance of accurate data and research in informing policy decisions

In the world of politics, making well-informed decisions is crucial. And when it comes to issues as contentious as pit-bull dog ownership, accurate data and research are paramount in shaping effective policies. Understanding the true impact of pit-bull dogs on public safety, the role of breed-specific legislation, and debunking myths and misconceptions surrounding these dogs requires a rigorous examination of the available evidence.

Accurate data and research play a vital role in shedding light on the reasons why pit-bull dogs should be banned. By analyzing comprehensive studies and statistics, policymakers can gain insights into the potential risks associated with pit-bull ownership. This information can help them better understand the dangers posed by these dogs and make informed decisions to protect public safety.

Moreover, accurate data and research are indispensable in assessing the correlation between pit-bull dogs and dog aggression incidents. By studying scientific findings and analyzing real-world cases, policymakers can gain a deeper understanding of the factors contributing to dog aggression and identify potential solutions. This knowledge can inform the development of effective policies aimed at reducing such incidents.

Accurate data and research also help to debunk myths and misconceptions surrounding pit-bull dogs. These dogs have often been unfairly stigmatized, leading to biased perceptions and misguided policies. By relying on credible research and scientific evidence, policymakers can challenge these misconceptions and ensure that their decisions are based on facts rather than unfounded beliefs.

Furthermore, accurate data and research shed light on the economic costs associated with pit-bull dog attacks. By quantifying the financial burden imposed on communities, policymakers can assess the impact on public resources and make informed decisions regarding the allocation of funds for prevention and intervention programs.

It is essential to explore potential alternatives to banning pit-bull dogs, and accurate data and research can provide valuable insights. By examining successful strategies implemented in other jurisdictions, policymakers can identify alternative approaches that promote responsible ownership and public safety without resorting to a blanket ban.

Lastly, accurate data and research help to counter the role of media sensationalism in shaping public perception of pit-bull dogs. Media portrayals often focus on isolated incidents, contributing to an exaggerated fear of these dogs. By relying on objective research, policymakers can challenge these sensationalized narratives and ensure that policy decisions are grounded in reality.

In conclusion, accurate data and research are indispensable in informing policy decisions regarding the banning of pit-bull dogs. By relying on credible evidence, policymakers can gain a comprehensive understanding of the impact of these dogs on public safety, debunk myths and misconceptions, explore alternatives, and develop effective policies that balance the interests of responsible dog owners and public welfare. Only through a rigorous examination of the available evidence can politicians make well-informed decisions that serve the best interests of their constituents.

Chapter 5: The ethical concerns surrounding pit-bull dog ownership

The ethical implications of breeding and perpetuating aggressive traits

In the ongoing debate surrounding pit-bull dogs and their potential danger to society, one aspect that cannot be ignored is the ethical implications of breeding and perpetuating aggressive traits within this breed. As politicians, it is crucial to consider the moral responsibility we have in ensuring the well-being and safety of our communities.

Breeding for aggression raises numerous ethical concerns. First and foremost, it goes against the principle of promoting empathy and compassion towards all living beings. By intentionally breeding dogs with aggressive tendencies, we are essentially creating animals that pose a heightened risk to both humans and other animals. This raises questions about our duty to protect innocent lives and prevent unnecessary harm.

Moreover, breeding for aggression perpetuates a cycle of violence and harm. Aggressive traits can be passed down from generation to generation, making it increasingly difficult to break this cycle. This not only jeopardizes public safety but also puts a strain on resources, as more incidents of aggression result in increased costs for medical treatments, legal actions, and animal welfare services.

Another ethical concern is the impact on responsible dog owners. While it is true that not all pit-bull dogs are aggressive, breed-specific bans can unfairly stigmatize responsible owners who have taken the necessary steps to ensure their dogs are well-behaved and trained. Banning a specific breed may punish responsible individuals who have invested time, effort, and resources into their pets, creating a sense of injustice.

Furthermore, breeding for aggression contradicts the principle of responsible pet ownership. Responsible owners prioritize the well-being and safety of their pets, as well as the community they live in. By creating and perpetuating aggressive traits within a breed, we are undermining the very foundation of responsible pet ownership and disregarding the potential harm it can cause to individuals and society as a whole.

As politicians, it is essential to address these ethical concerns when considering breed-specific legislation. While it is important to prioritize public safety, we must also balance this with the moral responsibility we have towards these animals and the impact on responsible owners. Exploring alternative solutions and investing in education and awareness programs may provide a more equitable approach to addressing the issue of dog aggression, without resorting to a blanket ban on specific breeds.

In conclusion, the ethical implications of breeding and perpetuating aggressive traits cannot be ignored in the discussion surrounding pit-bull dogs. As politicians, it is our duty to carefully consider these concerns and find a balanced solution that prioritizes public safety while also upholding principles of compassion, responsible pet ownership, and justice for responsible owners.

The responsibility of owners to properly train and socialize their dogs

In the contentious debate surrounding pit-bull dogs and whether they should be banned, one crucial aspect that often gets overlooked is the responsibility of owners to properly train and socialize their dogs. While it is true that certain breeds may have innate tendencies towards aggression, it is ultimately the owner's duty to ensure that their dog is well-behaved and poses no threat to public safety.

Proper training and socialization are essential for any dog, regardless of breed. However, due to the potential strength and power of pit-bull dogs, it becomes even more imperative for their owners to invest time, effort, and resources into their upbringing. By doing so, owners can help prevent any potential incidents or attacks that may occur due to a lack of training.

Training should begin at an early age and should focus on teaching basic obedience commands such as sit, stay, and come. Additionally, owners should work on teaching their dogs proper leash manners and how to interact appropriately with people and other animals. This socialization process is crucial, as it helps pit-bull dogs develop a positive association with different environments, situations, and individuals.

Owners should also consider enrolling their pit-bull dogs in obedience classes or seeking the assistance of professional trainers. These experts can provide guidance on how to address specific behavioral issues and ensure that the dog receives the necessary discipline and structure to become a well-rounded companion.

Furthermore, responsible owners should prioritize the physical and mental well-being of their pit-bull dogs. Regular exercise, mental stimulation, and a balanced diet are all essential components of a healthy dog's life. Neglecting these aspects can lead to frustration, anxiety, and potentially aggressive behavior.

Finally, owners must also take appropriate measures to prevent their dogs from escaping or becoming a danger to others. This may include securely fencing their property, using proper restraints when in public, and adhering to local leash laws. By doing so, owners can minimize the risk of their pit-bull dogs causing harm or becoming involved in potentially dangerous situations.

In conclusion, while the debate on banning pit-bull dogs continues to rage on, it is crucial to emphasize the responsibility of owners to properly train and socialize their dogs. By investing time, effort, and resources into their pit-bull's upbringing, owners can help prevent incidents and ensure the safety of both their dogs and the public. Proper training, socialization, and responsible ownership are key factors in mitigating the potential risks associated with pit-bull dogs and should be emphasized in any discussion on breed-specific legislation.

The ethical considerations of prioritizing public safety over personal preferences

The subchapter titled "The ethical considerations of prioritizing public safety over personal preferences" delves into the moral dilemmas that arise when making decisions regarding the banning of pit-bull dogs. This chapter aims to address politicians and highlight the importance of placing public safety above personal preferences in matters of breed-specific legislation.

As elected representatives, politicians have a responsibility to protect the welfare and well-being of their constituents. When it comes to pit-bull dogs, the evidence overwhelmingly points to their involvement in a disproportionate number of severe and fatal dog attacks. This poses a significant threat to public safety, particularly to vulnerable groups such as children and the elderly. Thus, prioritizing public safety becomes a matter of ethical obligation.

While some argue that banning pit-bull dogs infringes upon personal freedoms and choices, it is crucial to recognize that personal preferences should not override public safety concerns. The ethical dilemma here lies in striking a balance between individual rights and the greater good. By implementing breed-specific legislation, politicians can ensure the safety of their communities, even if it means restricting certain breeds.

Moreover, debunking myths and misconceptions about pit-bull dogs is essential to address the ethical concerns surrounding their ownership. Pit-bull dogs are often unfairly stigmatized due to media sensationalism and incorrect information. Politicians must encourage a rational and evidence-based conversation about pit-bull dogs to combat discrimination and promote responsible ownership practices.

Additionally, exploring potential alternatives to banning pit-bull dogs is an ethical imperative. This may include measures such as mandatory temperament testing, strict licensing requirements, and owner education programs. By implementing these alternatives, politicians can demonstrate their commitment to finding a balanced solution that considers both public safety and responsible dog ownership.

Ultimately, the ethical considerations of prioritizing public safety over personal preferences necessitate a comprehensive analysis of the impact of breed-specific bans on responsible pit-bull dog owners. While the ban may inconvenience responsible owners, it is crucial to weigh the potential risks to public safety against individual preferences. By addressing these ethical concerns and promoting evidence-based decision-making, politicians can make informed choices that prioritize the well-being of their communities while still respecting personal freedoms.

Chapter 6: The correlation between pit-bull dogs and dog aggression incidents

The scientific evidence linking pit-bull dogs to higher rates of aggression

Title: The Scientific Evidence Linking Pit-Bull Dogs to Higher Rates of Aggression

Introduction:

In order to make informed decisions regarding public safety, it is essential for politicians to consider the scientific evidence that links pit-bull dogs to higher rates of aggression. While it is crucial to acknowledge that not all pit-bull dogs are aggressive, research has consistently shown a correlation between this breed and aggression incidents. This subchapter aims to provide a comprehensive analysis of the scientific evidence supporting the case for banning pit-bull dogs.

1. Understanding Aggression in Pit-Bull Dogs:

Numerous studies have demonstrated that pit-bull dogs display higher levels of aggression compared to other breeds. Experts have identified a combination of genetic factors, such as selective breeding for aggression traits, and environmental factors, including poor socialization and training, that contribute to this tendency.

2. Aggression Incidents and Public Safety:

The impact of pit-bull dog aggression on public safety cannot be underestimated. Statistics reveal that pit-bull dogs are disproportionately involved in severe attacks, resulting in fatalities and life-altering injuries. By taking into account this scientific evidence, politicians can effectively address public safety concerns associated with pit-bull dogs.

3. The Effectiveness of Breed-Specific Legislation:

Breed-specific legislation (BSL) has been implemented in various jurisdictions as a means to reduce dog bite incidents. Studies analyzing the impact of BSL have shown mixed results. However, research does indicate that breed-specific bans can significantly decrease the occurrence of severe dog attacks when properly enforced.

4. Debunking Myths and Misconceptions:

Public perception of pit-bull dogs is often influenced by myths and misconceptions. This section challenges these misconceptions, using scientific evidence to dispel common myths such as "it's all in how they are raised" or "any dog can be aggressive."

5. Ethical Concerns Surrounding Pit-Bull Dog Ownership:

Ethical considerations arise when discussing pit-bull dog ownership due to the risk they pose to public safety. It is crucial for politicians to balance individual rights with the greater good, ensuring public safety remains a priority.

Conclusion:

Scientific evidence points to a correlation between pit-bull dogs and higher rates of aggression, an issue that demands the attention of politicians. By considering this evidence, policymakers can make informed decisions regarding the banning of pit-bull dogs, taking into account the impact on public safety, responsible dog owners, and potential alternatives to breed-specific bans. It is imperative to address this issue comprehensively and proactively, keeping the well-being of communities at the forefront of decision-making processes.

The role of genetics and breeding in shaping dog behavior

In the ongoing debate surrounding pit-bull dogs, it is crucial to consider the role of genetics and breeding in shaping dog behavior. Understanding these factors is essential for policymakers who are tasked with making informed decisions about whether or not to ban certain breeds.

Genetics play a significant role in determining a dog's behavior, and pit-bull dogs are no exception. Through selective breeding, certain traits have been emphasized in pit-bull dogs, including strength, tenacity, and loyalty. While these traits can make them excellent companions when properly trained and socialized, they can also become problematic if not responsibly managed.

Breeders have a significant influence on a dog's temperament and behavior through the selection of breeding pairs. Irresponsible breeding practices, such as breeding for aggression or neglecting proper socialization, can contribute to behavioral issues in any breed, including pit-bull dogs. It is important to acknowledge that not all pit-bull dogs exhibit aggressive behavior, and responsible breeding practices can help mitigate potential issues.

However, it is crucial to recognize that genetics alone do not determine behavior. Environment and socialization also play a crucial role in shaping a dog's temperament. Proper training, socialization, and responsible ownership are key factors in preventing dog aggression incidents, regardless of the breed.

While it is true that certain breeds, including pit-bull dogs, have been involved in a higher number of dog-related incidents, it is essential to avoid blanket assumptions and generalizations. Focusing solely on breed-specific legislation can overlook the underlying factors that contribute to dog aggression incidents. Instead, a comprehensive approach that considers responsible ownership, training, and socialization for all breeds is necessary.

Policymakers should also be aware of the potential unintended consequences of breed-specific bans. These bans can unfairly target responsible pit-bull dog owners and their well-behaved pets, leading to negative impacts on responsible dog ownership and the bond between humans and animals.

In conclusion, genetics and breeding play a significant role in shaping dog behavior, including that of pit-bull dogs. However, it is important to avoid breed-specific generalizations and focus on responsible ownership, training, and socialization for all breeds. A comprehensive approach that considers these factors will be more effective in reducing dog aggression incidents and ensuring public safety.

Understanding the potential impact of environment on dog aggression

In order to fully comprehend the issue of dog aggression, it is crucial to consider the potential impact of the environment in which dogs are raised and socialized. This subchapter aims to shed light on this aspect of the debate surrounding pit-bull dogs and their suitability as pets. By understanding the influence of the environment on dog behavior, policymakers can make informed decisions regarding the banning of pit-bull dogs.

Numerous studies have shown that a dog's environment plays a significant role in shaping its behavior. Factors such as socialization, training, and the presence of positive or negative stimuli can greatly impact a dog's propensity for aggression. It is important to note that aggression is not an inherent trait of pit-bull dogs, but rather a result of various environmental factors.

Proper socialization from a young age is crucial in preventing the development of aggressive behavior in dogs. Dogs that are exposed to a wide range of people, animals, and environments are less likely to exhibit aggression towards unfamiliar stimuli. Conversely, dogs that are isolated or subjected to negative experiences are more likely to display aggressive tendencies.

Training methods also play a vital role in shaping a dog's behavior. Positive reinforcement techniques, which reward desired behavior, have been proven to be highly effective in reducing aggression in dogs. Conversely, punitive training methods that rely on fear and intimidation can exacerbate aggressive tendencies.

Furthermore, responsible ownership and management practices can greatly reduce the likelihood of dog aggression incidents. Ensuring that dogs are properly contained, supervised, and receive adequate physical and mental stimulation are all crucial in preventing aggressive behavior.

It is important to recognize that any breed of dog, including pit-bull dogs, can exhibit aggression if not raised and socialized properly. By focusing solely on breed-specific legislation, policymakers risk overlooking the root causes of aggression and failing to address the issue effectively.

In conclusion, understanding the potential impact of the environment on dog aggression is crucial when considering the banning of pit-bull dogs. By promoting responsible ownership practices, implementing effective training methods, and encouraging proper socialization, policymakers can address the issue of dog aggression more effectively. It is essential to move beyond breed-specific legislation and focus on holistic approaches that consider the role of the environment in shaping dog behavior.

Chapter 7: The economic costs associated with pit-bull dog attacks

The financial burden on victims and their families

The financial burden on victims and their families is an often overlooked aspect of the pit-bull dog debate. While the physical and emotional toll of a dog attack is undeniable, the financial implications can be just as devastating.

When a pit-bull dog attack occurs, victims often require immediate medical attention. This can include emergency room visits, surgeries, and ongoing rehabilitation. These medical expenses can quickly add up, putting a significant strain on the victim and their family. In some cases, victims may also require long-term care or therapy to recover from their injuries, further increasing the financial burden.

In addition to medical expenses, victims may also face lost wages or even the loss of their job if their injuries prevent them from working. This loss of income can be particularly challenging for low-income families, who may already be struggling financially. The financial strain can also lead to increased stress and anxiety for the victim and their family, making the recovery process even more difficult.

Furthermore, there are often legal costs associated with dog attacks. Victims may choose to pursue legal action against the owner of the pit-bull dog, seeking compensation for their injuries and damages. However, navigating the legal system can be expensive, with attorney fees, court costs, and other associated expenses. This can further exacerbate the financial burden on the victim and their family.

It is important for politicians to consider the financial implications of pit-bull dog attacks when evaluating the need for breed-specific legislation. While some may argue against banning pit-bull dogs based on personal beliefs or emotional attachments to the breed, the financial costs cannot be ignored. By implementing breed-specific bans, municipalities can help prevent future attacks and reduce the financial burden on victims and their families.

Additionally, exploring potential alternatives to banning pit-bull dogs can also address the financial concerns. This could include stricter regulations on ownership, mandatory training and socialization programs, or increased penalties for irresponsible owners. By targeting the root causes of dog aggression and promoting responsible ownership, the financial burden on victims and their families can be reduced.

In conclusion, the financial burden on victims and their families is a significant aspect of the pit-bull dog debate. The costs associated with medical expenses, lost wages, legal fees, and other financial implications can be overwhelming. By considering these financial burdens and exploring alternatives to breed-specific bans, politicians can make informed decisions that prioritize public safety while also addressing the financial concerns of victims and their families.

The costs of medical treatment and rehabilitation

The costs of medical treatment and rehabilitation associated with pit-bull dog attacks are staggering and cannot be ignored. As politicians, it is crucial to understand the financial implications that these incidents have on our society and the individuals affected.

When a pit-bull dog attack occurs, victims often sustain severe injuries that require immediate medical attention. These injuries can range from deep lacerations and puncture wounds to broken bones and internal organ damage. The initial medical treatment alone can be exorbitant, as victims may require emergency room visits, surgeries, and extended hospital stays. The costs associated with these procedures can quickly escalate, burdening both the healthcare system and the victims themselves.

But the financial burdens do not end there. Victims of pit-bull dog attacks often require extensive rehabilitation to recover from their injuries. This may include physical therapy, occupational therapy, and psychological counseling. These services can be ongoing and may last for months or even years, resulting in significant expenses for the individuals and their families. Moreover, the long-term impact on the victims' quality of life and ability to work should also be considered. If they are unable to return to their jobs or require modifications to their work environment, there are further economic consequences for society as a whole.

Furthermore, the costs of medical treatment and rehabilitation extend beyond the victims themselves. Insurance companies, both private and public, bear a substantial portion of these expenses, leading to increased premiums for policyholders. Additionally, government-funded healthcare programs may also experience financial strain as a result of these incidents. The allocation of resources towards treating pit-bull dog attack victims detracts from other critical healthcare needs and can create a ripple effect throughout the healthcare system.

By recognizing the economic costs associated with pit-bull dog attacks, politicians can make informed decisions regarding breed-specific legislation. Banning pit-bull dogs can help prevent these incidents from occurring in the first place, thereby reducing medical expenses, rehabilitation costs, and the overall burden on our healthcare system. It is crucial to consider the financial implications when evaluating the need for stricter regulations and bans to ensure public safety and the responsible allocation of resources.

The strain on insurance companies and public resources

The strain on insurance companies and public resources caused by pit-bull dogs is a significant concern that needs to be addressed. Insurance companies are facing immense financial burdens due to the high number of dog bite claims involving pit-bull dogs. These claims often result in costly settlements, medical expenses, and legal fees, putting a strain on the insurance industry as a whole.

Public resources are also being stretched thin as a result of pit-bull dog attacks. Emergency services, such as ambulance and hospital resources, are frequently utilized when individuals are injured in these incidents. Additionally, animal control agencies and law enforcement must allocate significant time and resources to respond to and investigate these attacks. These demands on public resources come at a cost to taxpayers and detract from other essential services that could be provided.

The strain on insurance companies and public resources underscores the urgent need for breed-specific legislation targeting pit-bull dogs. By implementing bans or restrictions on the ownership of these dogs, policymakers can alleviate the financial burden on insurance companies and free up public resources for more pressing needs.

Critics argue that breed-specific legislation is ineffective and unfairly targets responsible dog owners. However, it is crucial to debunk these myths and misconceptions surrounding pit-bull dogs. Research has consistently shown that pit-bull dogs are responsible for a disproportionate number of severe dog attacks. Their unique combination of physical characteristics and genetic predisposition to aggression make them a significant public safety concern.

Furthermore, the ethical concerns surrounding pit-bull dog ownership cannot be ignored. While responsible owners may argue that individual dog behavior is more important than breed, the potential for harm cannot be overlooked. The safety and well-being of the general public must take precedence over the desires of a few dog owners.

In exploring alternatives to banning pit-bull dogs, it is essential to consider the economic costs associated with their attacks. These costs include medical expenses, legal fees, and increased insurance premiums for dog owners. Implementing breed-specific legislation would significantly reduce these costs, benefiting both insurance companies and the public.

In conclusion, the strain on insurance companies and public resources caused by pit-bull dogs is a pressing issue that necessitates action. By implementing breed-specific legislation, policymakers can alleviate the financial burdens faced by insurance companies and free up public resources for more important purposes. It is imperative to debunk myths and misconceptions surrounding pit-bull dogs and prioritize public safety over individual desires. The economic costs associated with pit-bull dog attacks further emphasize the need for breed-specific bans. Taking these steps will not only protect public safety but also ensure the responsible allocation of resources for the betterment of society.

The long-term economic impact on communities affected by pit-bull dog attacks

Pit-bull dog attacks have far-reaching consequences that extend beyond the immediate physical and emotional trauma experienced by the victims. These attacks can also have a significant long-term economic impact on the communities affected. It is crucial for politicians to understand the economic implications associated with these incidents when considering the need for breed-specific legislation and potential bans on pit-bull dogs.

One of the primary economic costs of pit-bull dog attacks is the burden on the healthcare system. Victims often require immediate medical attention, including emergency room visits, surgeries, and ongoing rehabilitation. The costs associated with these medical treatments can be substantial, placing a strain on local hospitals and healthcare providers.

Additionally, victims may require long-term psychological therapy to cope with the emotional trauma, adding further financial burden to the community.

Furthermore, pit-bull dog attacks can have a detrimental effect on property values. When a community becomes known for frequent dog attacks, potential homebuyers may be hesitant to invest in the area, leading to decreased property values. This can result in reduced tax revenue for the local government, impacting funding for essential services such as schools, infrastructure, and public safety.

Another economic consideration is the potential impact on tourism and local businesses. If a community gains a reputation for being unsafe due to pit-bull dog attacks, tourists may choose to visit other destinations, resulting in lost revenue for hotels, restaurants, and other local businesses. Additionally, residents may opt to move away from these areas, leading to a decline in population and further economic decline.

The long-term economic impact of pit-bull dog attacks extends to insurance companies as well. Insurance providers often face increased claims and payouts due to these incidents, leading to higher premiums for policyholders. This can place an additional financial burden on residents and businesses in affected communities.

It is essential for politicians to consider these economic costs when evaluating the need for breed-specific legislation and potential bans on pit-bull dogs. While the focus is often on public safety and the well-being of individuals, the long-term economic consequences cannot be ignored. By implementing measures to prevent pit-bull dog attacks, such as breed-specific legislation, communities can protect their residents, property values, and economic stability.

Chapter 8: The potential alternatives to banning pit-bull dogs

Promoting responsible ownership and education

Promoting responsible ownership and education is essential when discussing the topic of banning pit-bull dogs. While it is important to address the concerns surrounding these dogs, it is equally important to recognize the role that responsible ownership and education play in preventing incidents and ensuring public safety.

Responsible ownership starts with educating potential dog owners about the characteristics and needs of pit-bull dogs. Many misconceptions exist about these dogs, and it is crucial to debunk these myths and provide accurate information. By understanding the breed, individuals can make informed decisions about whether a pit-bull dog is the right fit for their lifestyle and home environment.

Furthermore, responsible ownership entails proper training and socialization for pit-bull dogs. Owners should be educated on positive reinforcement training methods, which focus on rewarding good behavior rather than punishment. This approach promotes a strong bond between the owner and the dog, resulting in a well-behaved and well-adjusted pet.

Alongside education, enforcing stricter regulations and guidelines for pit-bull dog ownership can also contribute to responsible ownership. This may include mandatory licensing, registration, and microchipping, as well as regular veterinary check-ups and vaccinations. These measures ensure that pit-bull dogs are properly cared for and monitored.

In addition to promoting responsible ownership, education is crucial in shaping public perception of pit-bull dogs. Media sensationalism often portrays these dogs in a negative light, perpetuating stereotypes and fueling fear. By providing accurate information through public campaigns and educational initiatives, policymakers can help dispel these misconceptions and foster a more balanced understanding of the breed.

While banning pit-bull dogs may seem like a quick solution to address public safety concerns, it is important to consider the potential alternatives. Breed-specific bans have been shown to be ineffective in reducing dog bite incidents, as they fail to address the root causes of aggression. Instead, a comprehensive approach that focuses on responsible ownership, education, and enforcement of existing laws is more likely to yield positive results.

In conclusion, promoting responsible ownership and education is crucial when discussing the topic of banning pit-bull dogs. By providing accurate information, enforcing stricter regulations, and shaping public perception through education, policymakers can address public safety concerns while also respecting the rights of responsible pit-bull dog owners. Ultimately, it is through responsible ownership and education that we can create safer communities for both humans and animals alike.

Implementing stricter regulations and licensing requirements

In order to effectively address the concerns surrounding pit-bull dogs and public safety, it is crucial for politicians to consider implementing stricter regulations and licensing requirements. These measures can play a significant role in reducing the risks associated with pit-bull dog ownership and enhancing public safety.

Stricter regulations would involve imposing specific criteria for owning pit-bull dogs, such as mandatory microchipping, spaying/neutering, and obedience training. These requirements ensure that pit-bull dogs are properly identified, sterilized, and trained, reducing the likelihood of aggression and unpredictable behavior. By enforcing these regulations, politicians can provide a safeguard against irresponsible ownership and reduce the chances of pit-bull dog attacks.

Licensing requirements are another vital aspect of controlling pit-bull dog ownership. By implementing a licensing system, politicians can ensure that only responsible individuals who meet certain criteria are allowed to own pit-bull dogs. These criteria may include passing a comprehensive knowledge test, demonstrating the ability to handle and control the breed, and maintaining appropriate living conditions for the dog. Licensing would also involve regular inspections to ensure compliance with safety and welfare standards.

Stricter regulations and licensing requirements can effectively address the concerns surrounding pit-bull dogs without resorting to a complete ban. By imposing these measures, politicians can strike a balance between public safety and responsible dog ownership. This approach acknowledges that not all pit-bull dogs are inherently dangerous, but rather emphasizes the importance of responsible ownership and proper training.

Implementing these regulations and licensing requirements would also have economic benefits. By reducing the risks associated with pit-bull dogs and preventing dog attacks, the costs associated with medical treatment, legal proceedings, and public safety measures can be significantly reduced. This not only protects the public but also saves taxpayer money.

In conclusion, implementing stricter regulations and licensing requirements is a crucial step in addressing the concerns surrounding pit-bull dogs. This approach ensures responsible ownership, enhances public safety, and reduces the economic costs associated with dog attacks. By adopting these measures, politicians can strike a balance between protecting public safety and respecting the rights of responsible pit-bull dog owners.

Encouraging breed-specific rescue and rehabilitation programs

One of the key arguments against a blanket ban on pit-bull dogs is the potential for breed-specific rescue and rehabilitation programs. While it is true that some pit-bull dogs may display aggressive behavior due to various factors such as poor breeding, lack of socialization, or mistreatment, it is important not to overlook the possibility of rehabilitating these dogs and giving them a second chance.

Breed-specific rescue programs focus on rescuing pit-bull dogs from abusive or neglectful environments and providing them with proper care and training. These programs aim to address the root causes of aggression and ensure that these dogs are given the opportunity to become well-adjusted, loving family pets.

Rehabilitation programs play a crucial role in transforming pit-bull dogs with behavioral issues into safe and manageable companions. These programs employ experienced trainers and behaviorists who work closely with the dogs, using positive reinforcement techniques to modify their behavior and address any underlying issues. By providing these dogs with a structured and nurturing environment, they can learn appropriate social skills and overcome their past traumas.

Encouraging breed-specific rescue and rehabilitation programs not only offers a lifeline to individual pit-bull dogs but also contributes to public safety. By addressing the root causes of aggression, these programs reduce the risk of future incidents and promote responsible pet ownership. They also provide support and resources to owners, helping them understand and manage their dogs' needs effectively.

Furthermore, breed-specific rescue and rehabilitation programs can also help dispel the myths and misconceptions surrounding pit-bull dogs. By showcasing success stories of rehabilitated pit-bull dogs living happily in loving homes, these programs challenge the stereotypes and negative perceptions that often contribute to breed-specific bans.

In conclusion, rather than implementing a blanket ban on pit-bull dogs, politicians should consider the potential for breed-specific rescue and rehabilitation programs. These programs have the ability to transform the lives of individual dogs, promote public safety, and challenge misconceptions about the breed. By supporting and investing in these initiatives, politicians can demonstrate a compassionate and evidence-based approach to addressing the issue of dog aggression.

Exploring targeted breeding practices to reduce aggression

In the ongoing debate surrounding pit-bull dogs, it is crucial to explore all possible avenues to address the concerns raised by politicians and various stakeholders. One such avenue is the exploration of targeted breeding practices to reduce aggression in pit-bull dogs. By focusing on responsible breeding and promoting traits that prioritize temperament and socialization, we can potentially mitigate the perceived risks associated with this breed.

Breeders play a pivotal role in shaping the behavior of pit-bull dogs. By carefully selecting breeding pairs with stable temperaments, breeders can significantly reduce the likelihood of producing aggressive offspring. Additionally, early socialization and proper training can further enhance a dog's overall temperament and reduce the risk of aggressive behavior.

It is important to note that aggression is not exclusive to any particular breed. Numerous studies have shown that aggression in dogs is influenced by a variety of factors, such as genetics, environment, and individual experiences. Therefore, targeting breeding practices to reduce aggression should extend beyond pit-bull dogs and encompass all breeds susceptible to aggressive behavior.

Implementing targeted breeding practices requires collaboration between breeders, veterinarians, and behavioral experts. By establishing guidelines and standards for responsible breeding, we can ensure that only dogs with desirable temperaments are used for breeding purposes. This approach can help break the cycle of aggression and promote the production of well-behaved and socially adapted dogs.

However, it is essential to recognize that breeding alone cannot completely eliminate aggression in dogs. Responsible ownership, which includes proper training, socialization, and ongoing education, is equally vital in shaping a dog's behavior. By advocating for responsible ownership practices, we can address the root causes of dog aggression and minimize the risks to public safety.

In conclusion, exploring targeted breeding practices to reduce aggression in pit-bull dogs is a potential solution worth considering. By promoting responsible breeding, early socialization, and proper training, we can work towards producing well-behaved and socially adapted dogs. However, it is crucial to remember that responsible ownership is equally important in ensuring public safety. By addressing both breeding practices and responsible ownership, we can take a comprehensive approach to mitigate aggression in all dog breeds, not just pit-bull dogs.

Chapter 9: The impact of breed-specific bans on responsible pit-bull dog owners

The challenges faced by responsible pit-bull dog owners

Responsible pit-bull dog owners face numerous challenges in today's society. As politicians, it is crucial to understand these challenges in order to make informed decisions about breed-specific legislation and the potential banning of pit-bull dogs. This subchapter aims to shed light on the difficulties responsible pit-bull dog owners encounter and provoke thoughtful consideration.

One of the primary challenges faced by responsible pit-bull dog owners is the negative public perception surrounding their beloved pets. Pit-bull dogs have been stigmatized due to media sensationalism, perpetuating misconceptions about their temperament and behavior. This leads to discrimination against both the dogs and their owners, making it difficult for responsible owners to find housing or obtain insurance coverage.

Moreover, responsible pit-bull dog owners often face ethical concerns surrounding their ownership. They are constantly under scrutiny to prove their dogs' good behavior and responsible care. This can be emotionally draining and unfair, as responsible owners should not be held accountable for the actions of irresponsible individuals who neglect or mistreat their dogs.

In addition, responsible pit-bull dog owners bear the economic costs associated with owning such a breed. They invest time and resources in training, socializing, and providing proper medical care for their dogs. However, these costs can increase exponentially due to breed-specific legislation, such as mandatory liability insurance or breed-specific licensing fees. These financial burdens disproportionately affect responsible owners who have no intention of engaging in illegal activities or promoting aggression.

Furthermore, responsible pit-bull dog owners are affected by breed-specific bans, which often target all dogs of a certain breed or appearance. These bans punish responsible owners who have diligently trained and socialized their dogs, as well as those who participate in activities such as therapy work or dog sports. Instead of focusing solely on specific breeds, policymakers should consider alternative approaches that focus on individual dog behavior and responsible ownership.

It is important for politicians to recognize the challenges faced by responsible pit-bull dog owners. By addressing the negative public perception, debunking myths, and considering alternative approaches to breed-specific bans, policymakers can work towards a fair and effective solution that promotes public safety without penalizing responsible owners. Responsible pit-bull dog owners deserve to be recognized for their commitment to their pets and their communities, rather than being subjected to unjust treatment and discrimination.

The potential unintended consequences of breed-specific bans

While breed-specific bans may seem like a logical solution to the perceived dangers of pit-bull dogs, they come with a range of potential unintended consequences that policymakers must consider. It is important to approach this issue with a comprehensive understanding of the broader implications of such bans.

One of the primary concerns is the impact on responsible pit-bull dog owners. Breed-specific bans can unfairly target law-abiding citizens who have carefully trained and socialized their dogs. These owners may face the heartbreaking choice of giving up their beloved pets or relocating to areas where their breed is not prohibited. This can lead to a loss of community cohesion and a sense of injustice among responsible dog owners.

Furthermore, breed-specific bans can create a false sense of security. By focusing solely on a specific breed, policymakers may overlook other factors that contribute to dog aggression incidents. It is essential to recognize that any breed of dog has the potential to display aggressive behavior if not properly trained or socialized. By narrowly focusing on pit-bull dogs, policymakers may divert attention and resources away from addressing the root causes of dog aggression.

Another unintended consequence is the potential for an increase in illegal breeding and ownership. When a breed is banned, it often drives the market underground, leading to the proliferation of unregulated and poorly bred dogs. This can result in a higher incidence of health and behavioral issues, exacerbating the very problems breed-specific bans aim to address.

Additionally, breed-specific bans can perpetuate stereotypes and fuel media sensationalism. The media often sensationalizes pit-bull dog attacks, leading to an unfair vilification of the breed and further stigmatizing responsible pit-bull owners. By focusing solely on banning specific breeds, policymakers risk perpetuating misconceptions and failing to address the underlying issues related to responsible dog ownership and public safety.

Instead of breed-specific bans, policymakers should consider alternative solutions that target responsible ownership and focus on education, training, and socialization for all dog breeds. By implementing comprehensive dog ownership programs, communities can address the root causes of dog aggression and promote responsible pet ownership without unfairly targeting specific breeds.

In conclusion, while the intentions behind breed-specific bans may be well-meaning, it is crucial to consider the potential unintended consequences. Responsible pit-bull owners should not bear the brunt of misguided legislation, and communities should focus on comprehensive solutions that address the broader issues surrounding dog aggression and public safety.

The importance of providing support and resources for affected owners

In the ongoing debate surrounding pit-bull dogs and their potential dangers, it is crucial for politicians to consider the impact that breed-specific bans may have on responsible pit-bull dog owners. While public safety must always be the top priority, it is equally important to acknowledge the rights and concerns of those individuals who have chosen to own these dogs.

Implementing a ban on pit-bull dogs without providing adequate support and resources for affected owners would be both unfair and ineffective. Many responsible owners have invested time, effort, and love into raising their pit-bull dogs, and they should not be punished for the actions of a few irresponsible individuals. It is essential to recognize that the vast majority of pit-bull dog owners are law-abiding citizens who prioritize the well-being and training of their pets.

By providing support to affected owners, policymakers can ensure that the transition to a breed-specific ban is as smooth as possible. This support can come in various forms, including educational programs, training resources, and financial assistance for those who may struggle to find suitable new homes for their dogs. By offering these resources, policymakers can effectively address the concerns of responsible owners and mitigate the potential negative consequences associated with a breed-specific ban.

Moreover, providing support and resources for affected owners can help address the ethical concerns surrounding pit-bull dog ownership. Many responsible owners view their dogs as beloved family members and may experience emotional distress when faced with the possibility of losing their pets. By offering support, policymakers can demonstrate empathy and compassion towards these individuals, fostering a sense of understanding and cooperation.

In addition to the moral imperative, there are practical reasons for providing support to affected owners. A sudden influx of surrendered pit-bull dogs can strain animal shelters and rescue organizations, potentially leading to overcrowding and increased euthanasia rates. By offering resources to owners, policymakers can help alleviate this burden and ensure that these dogs are placed in suitable homes rather than being left to languish in crowded shelters.

In conclusion, when considering the implementation of breed-specific bans, it is crucial for politicians to recognize the importance of providing support and resources for affected owners. By doing so, policymakers can address the ethical concerns surrounding pit-bull dog ownership, mitigate the negative consequences associated with bans, and ensure a smoother transition for responsible owners. Ultimately, by taking a comprehensive approach that considers the rights and concerns of all stakeholders, policymakers can work towards a solution that prioritizes public safety while also recognizing the value of responsible pit-bull dog ownership.

Chapter 10: The role of media sensationalism in shaping public perception of pit-bull dogs

The influence of media narratives on public opinion

In today's digital age, the media plays a significant role in shaping public opinion on various issues, including the topic of pit-bull dogs. The way in which the media portrays these dogs can greatly impact public perception and ultimately influence policymakers' decisions. This subchapter aims to explore the influence of media narratives on public opinion regarding pit-bull dogs.

Media sensationalism has a profound effect on public perception of pit-bull dogs. Sensational headlines and exaggerated stories of pit-bull attacks dominate the news, highlighting the breed's aggression and danger. As a result, the public often associates pit-bull dogs with violence and considers them a threat to public safety. However, it is crucial for politicians to recognize that media narratives are often distorted and fail to present a balanced view of the issue.

Debunking myths and misconceptions about pit-bull dogs is essential to provide a more accurate understanding of the breed. Contrary to popular belief, pit-bull dogs are not inherently aggressive. Numerous studies have shown that a dog's behavior is primarily influenced by its upbringing and environment, rather than its breed. Therefore, it is important to challenge the media's portrayal of pit-bull dogs as inherently dangerous and instead focus on responsible ownership and proper training.

The media's portrayal of pit-bull dogs also affects responsible owners who genuinely care for their pets. Breed-specific bans not only punish responsible owners but also fail to address the root causes of dog aggression incidents. Politicians must consider alternative solutions, such as stricter regulations on dog ownership, education programs, and increased penalties for irresponsible owners.

To combat the influence of media sensationalism, policymakers should critically analyze the effectiveness of breed-specific bans in reducing dog bite incidents. Research has shown that these bans have limited impact and often result in the displacement of aggression towards other breeds. It is crucial for politicians to base their decisions on empirical evidence rather than media narratives.

In conclusion, the influence of media narratives on public opinion regarding pit-bull dogs cannot be underestimated. Politicians have a responsibility to critically evaluate media portrayals, debunk myths and misconceptions, and base their decisions on empirical evidence. By doing so, policymakers can ensure that their actions are guided by reason, fairness, and a genuine concern for public safety.

The responsibility of media outlets in reporting dog-related incidents

Subchapter: The Responsibility of Media Outlets in Reporting Dog-Related Incidents

Introduction

The media plays a crucial role in shaping public perception and influencing policy decisions. When it comes to reporting dog-related incidents, especially those involving pit-bull dogs, media outlets have a responsibility to ensure accurate, unbiased, and responsible reporting. This subchapter explores the role of media outlets in reporting dog-related incidents and highlights the ethical concerns and potential consequences of sensationalism.

1. Accuracy and Objective Reporting

Media outlets have a responsibility to report dog-related incidents accurately, providing all relevant information and context. This includes accurately identifying the breed involved in an incident, as misidentification can perpetuate misconceptions and unfairly stigmatize certain dog breeds, such as pit-bull dogs. Objective reporting should focus on the facts, avoiding sensationalism and emotional language that can skew public perception.

2. Avoiding Sensationalism

Sensationalism in reporting dog-related incidents can lead to unwarranted fear and panic among the public. Media outlets should refrain from using exaggerated headlines, graphic images, or misleading statistics that create a distorted view of the actual risks associated with pit-bull dogs. Sensationalized reporting can breed prejudice and hinder informed decision-making by policymakers.

3. Providing Context and Expert Opinions

Media outlets should provide context for dog-related incidents, including information on the circumstances, dog ownership practices, and responsible pet ownership education. Additionally, seeking expert opinions from veterinarians, animal behaviorists, and responsible dog breeders can provide a balanced perspective and help dispel myths and misconceptions surrounding pit-bull dogs.

4. Promoting Responsible Ownership

Media outlets can play a vital role in promoting responsible dog ownership practices. By highlighting the importance of proper training, socialization, and responsible breeding, they can contribute to reducing dog aggression incidents. Reporting success stories of responsible pit-bull dog owners can also challenge negative stereotypes and showcase the potential alternatives to breed-specific bans.

5. Holding Media Outlets Accountable

Policymakers should consider holding media outlets accountable for biased reporting or sensationalism that misrepresents dog-related incidents. Implementing guidelines and standards for reporting can help ensure responsible journalism and prevent the spread of misinformation that may contribute to breed-specific bans.

Conclusion

Media outlets have a significant responsibility in reporting dog-related incidents, particularly those involving pit-bull dogs. By prioritizing accuracy, avoiding sensationalism, providing context, promoting responsible ownership, and being held accountable, media outlets can contribute to a more informed public discourse and help shape effective policies that prioritize public safety without unfairly targeting specific dog breeds.

The potential for biased reporting and its impact on policy decisions

In today's age of information overload, the media plays a significant role in shaping public perception and influencing policy decisions. However, it is important for politicians to be aware of the potential for biased reporting, especially when it comes to contentious issues such as pit-bull dog ownership. Biased reporting can have a profound impact on policy decisions, distorting the truth, and perpetuating misconceptions.

One of the reasons why biased reporting is a concern is because it can create a skewed narrative surrounding pit-bull dogs. Media sensationalism often focuses on isolated incidents of pit-bull attacks, leading to an unfair portrayal of the entire breed. This can result in fear and prejudice among the public, prompting calls for a complete ban on pit-bull dogs.

However, it is crucial for politicians to critically examine the evidence and not base their decisions solely on media sensationalism. Research has shown that breed-specific legislation, including pit-bull dog bans, is ineffective in reducing dog bite incidents. It is essential to consider alternative approaches that focus on responsible ownership and education rather than targeting specific breeds.

Furthermore, biased reporting can also have a detrimental impact on responsible pit-bull dog owners. Many individuals who own pit-bull dogs are responsible pet owners who provide a loving and safe environment for their pets. Yet, biased reporting can stigmatize and discriminate against these individuals, leading to unfair restrictions and limitations on their rights.

To make informed policy decisions, politicians must seek out unbiased sources of information and engage in open dialogue with experts in the field. It is crucial to debunk myths and misconceptions about pit-bull dogs and consider the ethical concerns surrounding breed-specific legislation. By doing so, politicians can ensure that their decisions are based on evidence and reason rather than media sensationalism.

In conclusion, biased reporting has the potential to greatly influence policy decisions regarding pit-bull dog ownership. Politicians must be aware of the distortions and misinformation that can arise from biased reporting and strive to make informed decisions based on evidence and reason. By critically examining the facts and engaging in open dialogue, politicians can ensure that their policies are fair, effective, and grounded in truth.

Chapter 11: Exploring the effectiveness of breed-specific bans in reducing dog bite incidents

Analyzing case studies and data from jurisdictions with breed-specific bans

In this subchapter, we delve into the crucial aspect of analyzing case studies and data from jurisdictions that have implemented breed-specific bans. By examining real-world examples, we aim to provide politicians with concrete evidence and insights into the effectiveness of such bans and their impact on public safety.

Case studies from jurisdictions that have implemented breed-specific bans offer valuable information on the outcomes of these policies. By examining data on dog bite incidents, attacks, and public safety statistics, we can better understand the correlation between pit-bull dogs and dog aggression incidents. This analysis will help politicians make informed decisions regarding the need for breed-specific legislation.

One key aspect to consider is the role of breed-specific legislation in pit-bull dog bans. By examining case studies, we can evaluate the impact of these laws on reducing dog bite incidents and improving public safety. This assessment will provide politicians with a comprehensive understanding of the potential benefits and drawbacks of breed-specific bans.

Furthermore, this subchapter aims to debunk myths and misconceptions about pit-bull dogs by presenting factual data and case studies. By separating fact from fiction, politicians can make evidence-based decisions concerning the breed-specific bans. This analysis will also address the ethical concerns surrounding pit-bull dog ownership, ensuring that politicians have a well-rounded understanding of the issue.

Moreover, we will explore the economic costs associated with pit-bull dog attacks. By examining case studies, we can quantify the financial burden placed on communities due to these incidents. This analysis will provide policymakers with insights into the potential economic benefits of implementing breed-specific bans.

Additionally, this subchapter will explore potential alternatives to banning pit-bull dogs. By studying case studies from jurisdictions that have implemented alternative approaches, such as education and responsible ownership programs, politicians can evaluate their efficacy in reducing dog bite incidents.

Lastly, we will critically examine the impact of breed-specific bans on responsible pit-bull dog owners. By analyzing case studies, we can assess the potential consequences of these bans on law-abiding citizens who own pit-bull dogs. This analysis will help politicians strike a balance between public safety and the rights of responsible dog owners.

In conclusion, analyzing case studies and data from jurisdictions with breed-specific bans is essential for politicians to make informed decisions regarding the banning of pit-bull dogs. By examining real-world examples, debunking myths, and exploring alternative approaches, this subchapter provides an evidence-based analysis of the effectiveness of breed-specific bans in reducing dog bite incidents and ensuring public safety.

Evaluating the impact on dog bite incidents and public safety

Dog bite incidents and public safety are crucial concerns that demand careful evaluation when considering the ban on pit-bull dogs. This subchapter aims to provide politicians with a comprehensive analysis of the impact that pit-bull dogs have on these issues. Understanding this impact is essential for making informed decisions regarding breed-specific legislation and ensuring the safety of our communities.

Pit-bull dogs have been frequently associated with dog aggression incidents, leading to concerns about public safety. However, it is important to debunk myths and misconceptions surrounding these dogs. Studies have shown that breed-specific bans often fail to address the root causes of dog aggression incidents. Instead, responsible ownership and proper training are more effective in preventing such incidents.

Moreover, it is crucial to consider the economic costs associated with pit-bull dog attacks. These incidents can result in substantial medical expenses, legal fees, and compensation claims. By examining these costs, policymakers can better understand the financial impact of pit-bull dog attacks on communities and explore potential alternatives to banning these dogs.

Breed-specific legislation, such as pit-bull dog bans, also raises ethical concerns. It is important to balance public safety with the rights of responsible pit-bull dog owners. A ban may unfairly penalize responsible owners who have properly trained and socialized their dogs. Evaluating the impact of breed-specific bans on these responsible owners will help ensure that any legislation implemented is fair and effective.

Media sensationalism plays a significant role in shaping public perception of pit-bull dogs. Biased or exaggerated reporting can perpetuate stereotypes and contribute to the negative perception of these dogs. By examining the role of media sensationalism, policymakers can gain a better understanding of the public's perception and make informed decisions based on facts rather than emotions.

Finally, exploring the effectiveness of breed-specific bans in reducing dog bite incidents is crucial. Studies have shown mixed results, indicating that such bans may not be the most effective solution. Evaluating alternative approaches, such as promoting responsible ownership, implementing stronger animal control measures, and increasing public education, can help reduce dog bite incidents in a more holistic manner.

In conclusion, evaluating the impact of pit-bull dogs on dog bite incidents and public safety is essential for policymakers when considering a ban on these dogs. By examining the correlation between pit-bull dogs and dog aggression incidents, the economic costs associated with pit-bull dog attacks, the role of breed-specific bans, and the effectiveness of alternatives, politicians can make informed decisions that prioritize public safety while being fair to responsible dog owners.

Considering alternative approaches and their potential effectiveness

As policymakers, it is crucial to explore alternative approaches and evaluate their potential effectiveness when addressing public safety concerns related to pit-bull dogs. While advocating for a complete ban on pit-bull dogs may seem like a straightforward solution, it is essential to consider other options that may achieve the desired outcomes while also preserving individual rights and promoting responsible dog ownership.

One alternative approach worth considering is the implementation of stricter regulations and licensing requirements for pit-bull dog owners. By imposing stricter guidelines, such as mandatory training and socialization programs, we can ensure that pit-bull dogs are raised in responsible and safe environments. This approach not only promotes responsible ownership but also addresses the root causes of aggression and potential public safety risks associated with these dogs.

Another potential alternative is the promotion of education and awareness campaigns. By providing communities with accurate information about pit-bull dogs, we can debunk myths and misconceptions that often lead to unwarranted fear and discrimination. Educating the public about responsible dog ownership, proper training techniques, and the importance of socialization can help prevent dog aggression incidents, regardless of breed.

Furthermore, investing in targeted interventions that focus on early identification and prevention of dog aggression can be an effective approach. By implementing behavior assessment programs and providing resources for owners to address any potential aggression issues, we can reduce the likelihood of dog attacks and improve public safety.

It is also essential to explore the potential of breed-neutral legislation. Instead of targeting specific breeds, legislation can focus on responsible ownership practices, regardless of the breed. This approach ensures that all dog owners are held accountable for their pet's behavior, regardless of breed, while also avoiding any discriminatory practices.

Lastly, conducting comprehensive studies and research on the effectiveness of breed-specific bans is crucial. While some argue that these bans have proven effective in reducing dog bite incidents, others question their validity and point out potential unintended consequences. By thoroughly analyzing the data and considering multiple perspectives, policymakers can make informed decisions and implement measures that truly enhance public safety.

In conclusion, while a complete ban on pit-bull dogs may be one option, it is essential for policymakers to consider alternative approaches and their potential effectiveness. Stricter regulations, education and awareness campaigns, targeted interventions, breed-neutral legislation, and thorough research should all be explored to ensure public safety while also respecting individual rights and promoting responsible dog ownership. By taking a comprehensive approach, policymakers can make informed decisions that address the concerns surrounding pit-bull dogs while achieving the desired outcomes for their communities.

The importance of ongoing evaluation and adjustment of policies

In the realm of public safety, it is crucial for policymakers to recognize the significance of ongoing evaluation and adjustment of policies. This holds true when considering the issue of pit-bull dog bans. As politicians, it is your duty to ensure that the laws and regulations put in place are effective, fair, and based on solid evidence.

Policies related to pit-bull dog bans must be subject to constant evaluation to determine their impact on public safety. It is essential to assess whether these bans are successfully reducing dog bite incidents and protecting communities. By conducting regular evaluations, policymakers can gather data and statistics to measure the effectiveness of breed-specific legislation. This information is invaluable in making informed decisions about whether adjustments need to be made to existing policies or if alternative measures should be explored.

One aspect that requires careful consideration is the correlation between pit-bull dogs and dog aggression incidents. Ongoing evaluation of policies can shed light on whether breed-specific bans are truly effective in reducing these incidents. It is important to distinguish between responsible pit-bull dog owners and those who engage in irresponsible ownership practices. Policies should be adjusted to target the latter group while protecting the rights of responsible owners who have properly trained and socialized their dogs.

Furthermore, ongoing evaluation allows politicians to address misconceptions and debunk myths surrounding pit-bull dogs. Media sensationalism often shapes public perception, leading to unfair stigmatization of this breed. By regularly assessing the impact of breed-specific bans on responsible pit-bull dog owners, policymakers can work towards fostering a more accurate understanding of pit-bull dogs and their behavior.

In addition to public safety concerns, the economic costs associated with pit-bull dog attacks must also be examined. Ongoing evaluation of policies can provide a comprehensive understanding of the financial burden imposed by these incidents, including medical expenses, legal costs, and insurance claims. This data can guide policymakers in making informed decisions about the allocation of resources and the implementation of preventative measures.

In conclusion, ongoing evaluation and adjustment of policies regarding pit-bull dog bans is of utmost importance for politicians. It enables policymakers to assess the impact of breed-specific legislation on public safety, debunk myths and misconceptions, and consider alternative measures. By conducting regular evaluations, politicians can ensure that their decisions are evidence-based, fair, and effective in reducing dog aggression incidents. Ultimately, the safety and well-being of communities should be the driving force behind any policy related to pit-bull dog bans.